Flawed Words and Stubborn Sounds

A CONVERSATION WITH *Elliott Carter*

Flawed Words and Stubborn Sounds

A CONVERSATION WITH *Elliott Carter*

≪-≪-≪-≪-

BY ALLEN EDWARDS

W · W · *Norton & Company* · *Inc* · *New York*

Note that . . . delight,
Since the imperfect is so hot in us,
Lies in flawed words and stubborn sounds.

Wallace Stevens (*The Poems of Our Climate*)

Contents

Foreword

The conversation presented to the reader in the following pages is a condensed, reordered, and partly rewritten transcript of a series of tape-recorded interviews between Elliott Carter and myself that took place at intervals over the period from 1968 to 1970. These interviews were undertaken at my suggestion, out of consideration for the fact that Elliott Carter remained too absorbed in his proper work as a composer to be able to devote the necessary time to recasting for publication in book form the notes he had made for a series of lectures he later gave as Ward Lucas Visiting Professor of Music at Carleton College in 1966. In view of the relative rarity and brevity of Elliott Carter's published writings since 1950 on music and musical life, it seemed to me especially undesirable that the thoughts which might have been set forth in a book version of these Ward Lucas lectures should go entirely unrecorded in consequence of circumstances of an essentially external kind.

In suggesting the interview format to Elliott Carter, on the grounds that its time-saving features imposed it as the one apparently practical means of securing a record of the thoughts in question, I was aware that its intrinsic informality presented many problems of consequence for the substance and structure of the ultimately resultant text. These problems I attempted from the outset to place under a sort of control by painstaking advance preparation and ordering of the questions I planned to ask—later finding, however, that the constantly mutating pattern of spontaneous association and reflection in the live interview situation itself prevented an ideally rigorous and continuous exposition of some of the complex musical issues raised. Attempting to compensate for this by a subsequent revision of the original interview transcripts, I was led to a number of compromises of form by what I found to be the impossibility of imposing, after the fact, an invariably logical sequence and always rhetorically smooth literary surface on the original interview materials without discarding much that was parenthetical to the larger context but nonetheless worth saving for its own sake. The defects that remain in the final text are ones for which I am motivated to ask the reader's literary indulgence because of my conviction of the overriding value of the perspective here gained on many perplexing problems of contemporary music generally, as well as on the working methods and life-experience of a composer I know I am not alone in regarding as the most important yet to have appeared in America.

I am indebted to the composer Stephen Siegel for his kindness in helping me to conduct two of the six interviews on which the following text is based.

ALLEN EDWARDS

New York, September 1, 1971

Flawed Words and Stubborn Sounds

A CONVERSATION WITH *Elliott Carter*

ALLEN EDWARDS: *To begin on a somewhat topical note, Mr. Carter, there has been much journalistic talk lately about the possible "impending end" of serious music as a public art in the United States—what with the near-bankruptcy of some of our major orchestras, the reputedly declining sales of serious music recordings, and the invasion of the somewhat "visible" part of contemporary musical activity by Madison Avenue while the less exploitable part is left to gather dust in universities. Considering these circumstances, do you feel that there exist in contemporary European societies, by contrast, kinds of institutional or other safeguards that would make the continued survival of music as both a serious and a living, public art more of a certainty than it begins to appear in this country?*

ELLIOTT CARTER: There is undoubtedly a European sociological pattern—though one that is not easy to define precisely and quickly—that leads many people to feel that serious music is one of the sources of cultural inspiration they get from the society in which they live. This feeling leads (for instance in Germany, where it is very widespread) to a quite strong and continuing desire not only to preserve the older works, but to keep up the cultural pattern by constantly encouraging the production of new works of high quality, which can be expected to have a similar effect on members of the society. The very pronounced desire of Central European society to maintain a high musical culture points to an agreement among many of its members that an enjoyment and appreciation of serious music, old and new, is one of the things that really makes them be who and what they are in themselves.

Now it is also true in Europe generally that this particular kind of cultural concern with serious music is especially char-

acteristic of a small intellectual group, which has traditionally
been respected because it provided a very useful articulation of
aims, feelings, and thoughts for the individual's inner and outer
lives. For this helped to give these lives, if not a zestful, at least
a satisfying direction and meaning. When this meaning no
longer seemed adequate, because of social change, it was re-
thought by the intellectuals and made to correspond to the new
social situation.

It seems to me that an élite patterned on that of Europe
(without, of course, a similar historical and cultural basis) did
exist in America up until the depression of the thirties. Since
then, however, this group, if it still exists, has lost much of its
power to give a single cultural style to American society—if it
ever really had it. Its role, like the role of education, had been
to point out certain possible directions American life might
take. The exalted prophecies of the founding fathers, of Lin-
coln, Emerson, and Whitman, express this in a sense, but with
what now seems little really convincing authority. For these
men assumed that their exhortations could have the same effect
on our society that similar ones had had in Europe—which may
have been true among certain small groups here but certainly
does not seem to have been so among the large population.

The deep pessimism of so many other American writers,
taking up one or another of the themes of de Tocqueville's
Democracy in America, expresses distress that this familiar Eur-
opean cultural pattern does not seem to obtain here. Perhaps
this is because of the heterogeneity of our population, combined
with an unwillingness to manipulate public taste on a cultural,
if not political and economic level. For the difference in aims
between the manipulation of public taste here and in Europe
has often been pointed out. Formerly, in Europe, obviously,
aristocrats wanted to impress by the quality of their living and
sought to give examples of what the good life could encompass.
Even today, the European mass media, in some countries, con-
tinue to act as educators and as arbiters of taste. The opposite
effect of the purely commercial aims of the American media
is self-evident, promoting as it does a continual deterioration
of the very abilities our education tries to promote, and reduc-

ing as many as possible to the role of passive consumers of objects commercially profitable to their producers. The constant growth of this process here makes our cultural future harder and harder to plan for with each succeeding year. In music, many are worried about whether or how long serious music can persist, since at the present moment the extraordinarily rapid expansion of the "popularity" of "popular" music apparently threatens to sweep away the actual values and pleasures, as well as the resultant prestige, that a small group derives from serious music, and thus makes this music less attractive for possible newcomers to it.

Would you consider it relevant to this question that today in Europe access to the higher government and civil service posts still tends to lie very much by way of a kind of university system which, among other things, tends to lead those who go through it to either an awareness of or a deference to the notion of music as a serious art—whereas in America, the personalities who become important in politics or who gain power as bureaucrats are very often people who, if they have been through a university at all, have gone through it as, say, economics majors and have no knowledge beyond the specific practical field with which they later come to deal in their official capacities— with the result that within the American governmental system there is little tacit agreement about and pressure toward reliable financial support for "the arts" and music in particular? Certainly one imagines that the tacit agreement of the people who run the BBC or the German radio stations on the intrinsic worthwhileness of things like serious music must have an effect on the way the budgets of these organizations are distributed such as to include serious music . . .

Well, one of the funny things about the situation in Europe and about using a word like "élite," as I have, to describe the people you've mentioned is that many of them were precisely the sort of people who were very important in many of the revolutions in Europe that overthrew the various *anciens régimes.* One thinks of men like Karl Marx and Lenin and Trotsky, who were extremely "unpopulistic" types, and of many less famous ones of similar intellectual cast, who were of central importance, as a group, in mounting and directing many European revolutions. Of course, one of the consequences of this state of affairs has been that, despite the overthrow of aristocratic élites at various times and places in Europe, an interest in serious music has persisted nonetheless, because the kind of people who had leading roles in the revolutions and became important functionaries in the new régimes, were people who knew about and valued serious music because of their previous intellectual background. It's obvious, for instance, in the case of the Soviet revolution, that the people who formed the first Soviet régime were from an educated élite and thus went right on encouraging serious music after the czarist régime was destroyed. The same thing happens today in Eastern Europe—in East Germany and Poland and Czechoslovakia and in all the countries which have primarily Marxist-trained people in their bureaucracies. These can't be compared to those forming what we sometimes condemn as an established élite here, for they have a genuine respect for the arts. Serious music lovers in our country are sometimes unjustly associated with this Establishment élite of ours—unjustly, I say, because the arts have a broader, more far-ranging appeal, as we see in some of the Eastern countries and elsewhere, that separates them from (and indeed often opposes them to) the specialized class interests of one narrow-minded economic and social group.

Of course, in America it is certainly true that the kind of specialized education people get prevents them from developing a wider view of civilization and culture, to such an extent that when people who've been educated this way get into positions of political power they are not often interested or able to do anything very important to help the arts, which in every society need a certain amount of subsidy.

I must say, though, that beyond any question of politicians and bureaucrats there's the fact that, compared to the United States, Europe is a very densely populated area of the world and has been that way for a very long time. As a result, the very idea of education has a far deeper meaning there than over here—in the sense that, for example, Americans could always get up and go off somewhere else to change their lives and their whole situation, because there was always room in another place for another way of behavior, and it wasn't always so very necessary for them to solve problems because those could be side-tracked or side-stepped. In Europe this has not been so for many centuries, and, as a result, people had to be very smart and very clever and well-trained, figure out many ways of behaving, and foresee how other people would react to their ways of thinking—all of which has fostered a very highly intellectualized attitude on the part of a very large number of people, even of people who are not especially educated. They have a very strong social awareness, and this in itself encourages just the kind of thing that serious music caters to—that is, a society of people very aware of the reactions of other people. Ensemble music obviously presents this in a very clear way.

Aside from this, music was also something that people could cultivate within small family circles, while in America, where the family was much less "tight" and is becoming less and less so, music was not cultivated the way that it was in Europe. This seems to me a very important aspect of this question, because music was part of a social and family pattern that was rather static for a very long time in every European country, while in America it was not focused at all.

Another point is that Americans not only came from different places in Europe, with different kinds of musical traditions, but were also themselves a certain type of people, who were self-chosen to come here, and were frequently not the kind of people particularly interested in the arts. Generally, Europeans interested in the arts stayed at home, because they were sure the arts were very much better there. One thinks of Lorenzo da Ponte, who had to come to the United States for "moral" reasons—I doubt he would ever have come here, back in those early days, for any other.

Another aspect of the vast and obvious difference between the United States and Europe in the question of music is the fact that many, many people in Europe show deference to the idea that serious music is a good thing by paying for it out of their taxes, even though only a tiny proportion of them seem to participate very directly in serious music themselves. This is shown in a somewhat shocking statistic quoted in an American record magazine some time ago, which stated that the average total Western European sale of a given classical music recording was around 2,500 copies. Now, compared with the total population of Western Europe this 2,500 figure naturally appears ludicrously small. Yet, on the other hand, in America, where the circulation of classical music records is certainly much greater than that, still the trend in the past five years has been a diminishing one, as has also been the case in the area of the journalistic attention paid to serious music compared with popular music. In this light, it is interesting to consider the story in which the 2,500 figure mentioned above was quoted: according to this story, a European record company decided that, in order to increase the circulation of their classical records and encourage more people to become interested in serious music in general, they would arrange to have a given classical record broadcast by a popular-music station several times a day over a two-week period without any announcement concerning the record—that is, without identifying it as "classical music" or mentioning who wrote it or when it had been written, and so forth—this in order to reach people who were presumably intimidated by the "highbrow," "upper-class" atmosphere in which serious music was usually presented in concerts and over the state radio systems. The record was played sandwiched in between popular numbers without warning listeners of what was happening. Then, after two weeks it was finally announced what this piece was and who wrote it and that the recording was available in record stores. The result of this tactic was that this record has sold 70,000 copies to date . . .

Well, this is just like the popular music setup, in the sense that it seems *whatever* is played over the media a great many times ends up selling 70,000 copies, whereas if it's only played two or three times or not at all, it sells 2,500 copies.

Yet here one finds the Madison Avenue method placed in the service of something worthwhile . . .

Certainly, in this particular and unusual case. Yet this all revolves around the problem of an essentially passive public which buys records and wants to hear music on the basis of its familiarity rather than on the basis of its quality or even of the style it's written in. That is, I'm not sure just what this story signifies about the question of public taste and its being influenced by such means significantly for the better. I don't know that this indicates anything more than that this public became very familiar with a particular piece—which happened in this instance to be a classical piece. Whether, if this public became familiar with, say, *five* such pieces of serious music, they would then branch out and buy five other ones that hadn't been served up to them by the media, I would begin to question. I'm not sure, for example, whether the records of Bach sell any better than before, now that we have a "switched-on Bach" record, or whether the Mozart concertos in general sell any better since the *Elvira Madigan* business. What seems to happen is *not* that people's tastes are changed or that they are motivated to go exploring for themselves in the field of which they've been given a glimpse, but rather that they buy *only* the items that are directly plugged by the media from one month to the next and, indeed, are just as content with Elvis Presley as with the given Mozart piece—these having in common their fashionable momentary promotion by media, which dispense the listener from any effort of active searching, discrimination, and thought.

Still, one wonders whether the tactic adopted by the European record company might not have a beneficial effect if it were employed widely in the United States—given that very often a person's interest in something becomes bit by bit independent of the often extraneous influence that plays a role in making him pay attention to the thing in the first place. Certainly, for example, many people really do *come to like many classical pieces independently of the "star performers" who play a role in putting these pieces across in the first instance to the average listener, comparable to the role played by radio in putting over pieces of popular music.*

It is true that the situation today amongst classical music listeners is in many ways much better than it was throughout most of the nineteenth century when the cult of the performer and the attendant circus atmosphere were often more pronounced. But what has happened is that—as a result of the more serious atmosphere of, say, symphony concerts today, compared to the days of Liszt and Paganini—many people who would have gone to classical music concerts in the last century won't go any more. These are the kind of people who in the old days were brought into concerts because they had a lot of "pop" stuff on every program regardless of what else was on it. It was as if today the New York Philharmonic were to program a piece of Schoenberg and have it followed by an appearance of the Beatles or some other such outfit.

Yet, as you pointed out before, the popularity of a given piece or style of music, whether it be today the Beatles in the West or, say, Penderecki in Poland, has had to do with how strongly a given piece or kind of piece is put across either by live performances or by media—such that the public's taste ultimately, seems to reflect, more than to guide, the activities of performers and managers. At least this would seem to be the case if one considers that in Poland—where the radio is controlled by intellectuals who believe in serious music and who, therefore, promote heavily the works of serious contemporary Polish composers— Lutoslawski and others are popular with the music public in a way that no serious modern composer is in America, where the media are controlled by people who don't believe in serious music.

The popularity of the serious composers in Poland benefits very much from the fact that their activities are flagrantly in contradiction to the official Russian line on art—such that many Poles who wouldn't pay attention to Penderecki if he and they were in the American situation *do* pay attention to him because he and the others are part of a sort of anti-Russian "underground" even though they are officially sanctioned by the Polish government. In this respect, these composers appear as sort of New Leftists and, therefore, draw a lot of extramusical attention —in just the way that pop music groups in the West do if they merely proclaim themselves "anti-Establishment."

Of course, in Russia the case of Shostakovich might suggest that the championing and promotion of a serious composer by state-controlled media was in itself sufficient to put the composer across to a relatively sizeable public. Nonetheless, while it *is* true that Shostakovich is undoubtedly better known and more often played in Russia than he would be without state assistance, still he is not encouraged to write his best music by the official Soviet music apparatus, and he thus occupies quite an ambiguous position in relation to the question we're discussing. This is because the Soviet music bureau wants to have composers write "morally up-lifting" or folkloristically entertaining pieces which can stimulate the general Russian public's patriotism and moral adherence to the Soviet régime and its goals. Now, to the extent that, say, Shostakovich's music has not fed into these officially sanctioned aims, the official approval and support he has received has been withdrawn, while composers like Edison Denisov, who never write "official" music, have an even worse time of it, I think, than a serious composer in America usually does. This all boils down to the fact that Russian musical bureaucrats tend to support the kind of music which serves the régime, just as the musical bureaucrats in Poland, while somewhat more sophisticated than those in Russia, see that the purposes of the Polish national régime are, within limits, quite well served by "anti-Soviet music"—which just happens to be of a relatively progressive stamp, and which of course can also pass for "antibourgeois" music of a sort. In America these factors are not at work at all in the same sense—one can hardly imagine the election of Mr. Nixon or Mr. Humphrey being affected by a twelve-tone piece of some kind . . .

In any case, what one sees in Eastern Europe is not only a situation where the media are controlled by somewhat more intellectual people than we find in similar positions in America, but also one where political considerations are operative, sometimes to the detriment and sometimes to the benefit of serious contemporary music, for this music is in any case an important matter to the people in power.

Given that in America the media would seem to be controlled by those with the money to buy expensive air time and

thus would seem to be subject to an indirect form of élite manipu-
lation parallel to the obvious élite control which especially ob-
tains in Eastern Europe, and further given that the corporate
élite which appears to dispose of the content of American media
is quite indifferent to the fate of serious music, do you feel
that, in order to counterbalance this bias-by-default and the
consequent brainwashing of the general public in the direction
of trash music, it might be worthwhile for foundations to pur-
chase blocks of air time in which serious contemporary music
could be broadcast frequently enough to begin to reach a
wider public than it does through the restricted live concert
setup and through the very unsystematic broadcasting of re-
corded contemporary musical works which goes on presently?

Well, this might help, yet I really feel the problem lies
in our education, which does little to encourage the intellectual
curiosity, varied interests, and adventurous attitude that lead one
to be on the lookout for things the media don't serve up directly.
It often seems, in any case, as if the educational system here
does little to counter a purely passive, incurious, and uncritical
attitude to practically everything beyond the most immediate
utilitarian concerns and pursuits, so that what the media broad-
cast is taken flatly to be "all there is" to be interested in, enter-
tained by, or concerned with.

I'm certain, for instance, that if it bothered the general public
to be fed the pablum served by the media, the media would be
forced to broadcast something else because no one would watch
or listen, and the advertisers would have no market and no reason
to pay for radio and television programs. The fact that so many
people here are only too content with the typical offerings of
the mass media rests, as I have implied, on the fact (it seems to
me) that the basic vision of what it is to get an education and
to use it has been completely diluted in this country—in fact,
rather destroyed, in my opinion. Now this may be because
education has had to be so widely expanded. We've had the
problem in music, I think, just as in education, namely, that
with the rapid growth in the economy every operation be-
comes very much more expensive, and those operations that are

geared to make money do make more and more money, while those operations whose main end is not to make money, but, let's say, to improve the population's ability to think, its health, the cleanliness of the air, and so forth, become exorbitantly expensive because their costs keep pace with those that obtain in money-making operations. This leads to their costing so much that they become less and less well done, or else practically impossible, especially in cases like symphony orchestras and opera houses.

Of course, in America, the point of view on education of someone who has both attended a university and, in general, had the benefit of comfortable material circumstances naturally is very different at the outset from the point of view of someone who has not been as well off and who therefore tends to view education in a purely utilitarian way. This situation does not seem to be anything at all recent in American history, but rather points up precisely the traditional American point of view—distinct from the European—to wit, that education and educational institutions do not exist in or for themselves, or especially for the benefit of a tiny élite like the European one, but rather exist to help everybody at all levels help themselves to a better life—that help *and the proximal meaning of* better *being defined by the circumstantial point of departure of each individual, which, in the nature of things up to now, has been a modest one for a majority of people.*

Yet, the curious thing about all this is that the educational system not only has had to cater, for the most part, to the non-intellectual aims of many who were less well off but has been geared, almost exclusively, at every economic level to the idea of teaching people to make more money. At least until very, very recently, this seems to have been the underlying point of view of most wealthy young men going to Harvard quite as much as of most poor ones on scholarships at CCNY. This would certainly seem to account for the fact that in America there has not developed a significant intellectual group or attitude, even among those in advantageous economic circumstances. That is, in America, unlike Europe, a difference of fortune has not seemed to

mean the kind of difference of aim and outlook that would permit
a high culture to take root and grow securely, over and beyond
the economic life that naturally preoccupies most people, espe-
cially those who have not yet achieved a comfortable socioeco-
nomic position and justifiably make demands for a kind of educa-
tion which will help them to do so. This is why is seemed to me
when I was at Harvard that the few who came there really to get
an education in the arts, philosophy, or the pure sciences were in-
volved in some very tenuous and fantastic activity which had
literally nothing to do with what interested most other people,
even at Harvard—to say nothing of the surrounding society as
a whole. And I think even today, at a time when much larger
numbers of people go to universities and are interested in extra-
economic concerns than ever before, that such people have just
this same feeling of disconnection from the activities respected by
society as a whole, this same impression of being involved in
a world of experience that many others regard as fantastic and
unreal. This is certainly a partial cause of the unrest that has made
itself more and more felt on college campuses in very recent
years.

*In this connection, one interesting difference between Eur-
ope and America has traditionally been that members of élites
in Europe have usually felt no compunction whatever about
being in an élite and generally felt perfectly free to ignore
completely what in America would be considered the central
social activity, namely, the economic activity. Thus, someone
like Gide, for example, could live until he was fifty and never
once condescend to notice the existence of anything outside
literature, until one day, while on a "grand tour" of the Tchad,
he stumbled across the things that were going on in the French
colonies then. Whereas, on the contrary, the social pressure
on Henry James was enough to force him to leave America prac-
tically on a permanent basis, just so he could feel freer to be
the artist he was and not be sniped at socially for not being in
business or for not peddling sermons in his books.*

Yes, this certainly was true up until the later twenties in
Europe, and sometimes even now; yet what you notice more

recently is that intellectuals in Europe, like Sartre or Simone Weil, who were or are *ipso facto* members of an élite, have been much more intellectually penetrating in their criticism of the élitist *status quo* than writers in America, where the awareness of social inequality has traditionally been more immediate than it was in Europe before 1930. And certainly this state of affairs leads me to think that the European response to the problems of the age of technology and of the desire of people to improve their social and material conditions is likely to be a much more reasoned one in clarifying ends and means than is likely to be forthcoming in America, where an increasing number of issues have taken on the aspect of a brute conflict of forces unable to clarify their intentions sufficiently to act effectively.

Of course, while all of what has just been said might seem far removed from music and the problems surrounding it, nonetheless, the apparently simple, practical questions of where, for example, orchestras in America are going to get the money they will need merely to keep operating, as well as the question of why something like this should be a serious problem at all in a country as rich as America, naturally lead one fairly directly into broad questions of the kind we have been discussing. Still, the facts are that in a short space no "complete analysis" of these problems is possible and that even once analyzed the problems seem to remain largely intact and, indeed, come to appear more and more insoluble . . .

Well, as I said, and as many others have pointed out in recent times, the cost of music—and especially the cost of musical performance—increases with the economic demands of musicians, who feel they ought to be paid wages at least comparable to those paid to other professionals. But while wages of this latter kind have increased because of a technologically permitted increase in the productivity of labor, no increase in the "productivity" of a musician's labor is possible because there is no room for technology and its increased efficiency in the field of musical performance except for recordings and broadcasts. Thus, musical costs rise in an otherwise static situation, because one can't compensate by raising ticket prices more than a certain amount, just as one can't increase the size of audiences for individual concerts more than so much, nor the size of the classical or serious musical audience as a whole for recordings, et cetera, in any rapid way, due to the cultural problems discussed before.

This means that *unless* the restricted audience for serious music, whether live or recorded, is made up mainly of wealthy people—which nowadays it certainly is not—serious music will either have to be subsidized by the government or else be allowed to shrink down to a tiny level of activity. And given the increasingly pressing social problems and claims on government money today, it is certainly a question whether there will be any money available to support the large-scale orchestral enterprises in the future in the United States.

To be sure, this does not in any way mean that there is a decline of interest in serious music—there may even be an increase. What is does mean, though, is that the interest does not overlap to the necessary extent with private wealth and at the same time is not large enough to form the kind of political constituency necessary to gain a government subsidy. Thus, one can imagine the serious muscal life of America twenty years hence as being confined essentially to people's living rooms, where they would listen to recordings, made in places like Japan, of the music they want to hear. This would be because it would by then be economically feasible to make such recordings only in places where the costs were lower or a subsidy available.

Of course, it may be just barely possible that for reasons of international prestige—since this seems to be more important than home consumption—the government might finally decide to subsidize perhaps the so-called "big five" orchestras, which have a long-standing international reputation and whose disappearance would reflect poorly on the United States in the eyes of European countries (we have seen this happen already with many soloists and ensembles who are subsidized to play on foreign tours but not here). Yet, even if such a subsidy were finally forthcoming in the case of orchestras, it would have to help them exist here as well as tour abroad, and this would have to be justified by drawing to concerts larger and larger numbers of subsidizing taxpayers to hear the old familiar (but to them unfamiliar) war-horses of classical music. Now, while honorable enough in itself, such a program would mean little or nothing for contemporary music, and it seems to me that interest in the old war-horses cannot last, even where newly developed, unless there is contemporary music to provide new experiences free from the museum odor that automatically rises more and more strongly from the "standard repertoire" in the context of our present world-experience. Thus, the newly subsidized orchestras would have no future with this kind of setup and would soon find themselves again in a very deteriorated situation. But then America has always lived musically in a very deteriorated situation—we have always depended, and still do, on European government support and time and effort for our musical life over here, whether it be in the form of foreign musicians and composers exported and publicized by their own countries, or in the form of the musical education, performances, and recordings that many Americans have gone to Europe to get.

Of course, there's the fact that for orchestras to gain and maintain the cooperation of a good conductor they have to allow him a certain amount of freedom, and it seems that today, at long last, a few conductors are beginning to show some personal interest in contemporary music . . .

Well, there are some who are showing interest to see whether the public will follow, and if the public doesn't follow right away, with numerous *succès de scandale* and so on, most of these conductors can be expected to drop contemporary music like a hot potato in a very short time.

When you come to think about it, it's obvious that the first sign of trouble with the orchestras in America began to show up even before the Second World War, in the late thirties. Then the American orchestras began getting conductors who were "good showmen," and thus attracted an audience that had not previously gone to concerts. This immediately tended to change the concert atmosphere back in the direction of what it had been in the Liszt-Paganini days, with the cumulative result that we now have audiences who don't like to see a conductor who is not a "good showman." Thus today, if we have conductors who start to revolt against this peculiar kind of showmanship business, we will probably have to struggle very, very hard to find a new public. This will be quite difficult because obviously one can't just switch from one public to another in between subscription seasons at the New York Philharmonic—there are bound to be several seasons when the subscriptions will fall off very much while the Philharmonic is trying to find another audience. This problem, I might add by way of example, is reflected in the fact that, when I was at Harvard, *all* the students who were at all interested in music at Harvard subscribed to the Boston Symphony, while in recent times it seems no Harvard student would be caught dead at the Boston Symphony. They go occasionally, when there's some special thing that's unusual, but as a rule they don't go because they don't think the programs are interesting enough to be worth subscribing to.

Of course, things have improved somewhat over the situation ten years ago in the sense that now, if an orchestra sandwiches in a modern piece on a traditional program, the audience usually will be fairly quiet and won't just walk out in a rage.

Audiences are funny about modern music. On the brighter side, I've had experiences of audiences not being so much against it as against bad performances of it. I can remember that when Rosbaud came to the Philharmonic in 1960 or so and did an all-modern program—including the Schoenberg Five Pieces, Op. 16, and the Webern Six Pieces, Op. 6—the audience liked it very much and was enthusiastic, though it was the same old audience they always have. It's just that the music was played very well and convincingly. But what we've had year after year have been conductors not interested in contemporary music, who nonetheless feel they have to play it occasionally, but who don't have their hearts in it, nor do they have enough of an imaginative or musical grasp of most new scores to get the best out of them. As a result, they don't put the piece across, the audience and orchestra don't like it, and the whole thing is just a mess.

Another problem is that conductors lately have been choosing contemporary works of uncertain quality that run the risk of putting most of the audience off. They do this out of a sense of duty to be widely representative, to give unfamiliar, especially young composers a chance—which they should. But this has to be done with great circumspection so as to avoid alienating the audience completely. What is essential is to play a large proportion of recognized *good* works of contemporary music in order to get the audience interested in contemporary music, and only then, in this context, to play occasionally other kinds of works where the risk of losing the audience is greater. But to play *exclusively*, in the way of contemporary music, works of much less than first-rate quality just puts the audience off right at the start.

Aside from these practical questions concerned with contemporary music's performance and transmission to the public, another of the social questions connected with contemporary music is certainly the personal relation between the composer and the culture in which he grows up. One of the questions that used to be debated a great deal was just what serious American music might be, as distinct from serious European music. Today, in hearing the vastly different works of composers such as Ruggles, Ives, Varèse, Sessions, and Copland—to name only a few members of the pre–World War II generation of American composers— one can immediately tell that somehow none of this music could have been written in a European context, despite the obvious roots these works have in the European tradition of serious music. At the same time it is difficult to pinpoint in words just what these composers and their works, different as they are, have nonetheless in common that tells one they are no longer, so to speak, in the European esthetic frame . . .

Well, it's true that it's difficult to put your finger on national characteristics in music, even though these characteristics may be very obvious when you hear the works. It's obvious that, different as they are, Berlioz and Debussy have a quality that brings them together at the same time that it separates them from Schubert and Bruckner, and vice versa. Again and again in this music, one finds that French concern with clarity of texture, clarity and simplicity or elegance of gesture, and so on, which makes a very different impression from the German and Austrian concern for a kind of blurred warmth and intensity of expression.

In American music I would say one doesn't have quite the feeling one gets from practically all the important European works, the feeling that the means used by the composer to achieve his ends are ones that are, so to speak, worked over and focused in advance—not only by the composer himself, but by a whole historical community of composers all working in a somewhat similar direction and all sharing certain fundamental esthetic and linguistic assumptions. One is aware, in listening to representative works of American music, that these have not been produced in the atmosphere of intense activity, constant and intelligent intra-professional criticism, and regular contact among composers and between them and a sophisticated public that has helped give European music its particular honed and "finished" character.

On another level, American works are seldom the product of working methods characteristic of many important European composers, who have gone about their task in a systematic way, carefully coordinating musical means and ends at every level while weeding out initially accepted elements that did not contribute to their specific intentions. For often it seems that they must have formed a very clear idea of what they wished to accomplish, and were determined to pursue this down to the smallest details of their work. In my opinion, it is the very absence of this sharpness of focus and close coordination of means in terms of a very clarified musical intention that gives the good works of American music their special freshness and makes the listener sense in them an esthetic point of view different from the more or less standard European one. This difference of approach is evident in American art outside the field of music —most obviously, for instance, in the works of Poe and Whitman, both of whom explore new territory in which coordination of means and ends is not standardized. Poe, especially, it is my impression, was very conscious of trying to coordinate the different aspects of his works systematically. Whether he really constructed his works as he describes or not, and how much these depend for their effectiveness on his calculations, remain fascinating questions. In any case, Poe, Whitman, and Melville didn't coordinate their works in the almost "pat" way we expect from European artists. In this they point up what may be the most interesting and characteristic thing about American arts—namely, the adventurous interrelation between the materials used and the unexpectedness of their general development. Now, I think this comes simply from living in our society itself, though there was a time when many of us felt this should be thought out. We wanted to be "American" and to make it very clear to everyone that we were American composers, so we attempted to use various folkloric and popular-music elements to make our music have an "American" character. But, in my own case, I soon began to realize that this was unsatisfactory—in fact, that just being an American was already enough, that whatever American character my music had would be the character of myself making my music, and that it didn't matter what choice I made except to write the music I *most* wanted to write. *That*, I believed, would be American music. For I came to realize that America itself is being created right here before us, moment by moment, combining its sometimes perplexing unwillingness to consider the past with its good-natured generosity and idealistic hope for the future. To chart a cultural development here, it seemed to me, was a waste of time, while what was and is important is to make the present, with all its connections to the past and anticipations of the future, exist more powerfully than either of these. In this one doesn't just start systematically inventing a future America, but rather one makes it exist now. This is because America and being American are not, so to speak, pre-established or even analyzed ideas to which one conforms or really can conform. It is this that marks us as being very different from Europe—there, there *is* a pre-established idea of what it is to be a Frenchman for instance, and while of course many Frenchman don't conform to this idea, nonetheless they all have some version of the ideas of Descartes and Pascal and others in their background, which by itself has a distinct influence on what they themselves are.

Taking this thought further, one feels that, while the very same body of European musical precedent is available to Americans as to Europeans of the present time, still the "immanence"

of this body of precedent as precedent is in some sense less con-
straining here than in Europe; that is, one not only feels, in hear-
ing an American work, that, as you say, many more unexpected
kinds of things could easily happen than would be likely in a
comparable European work, for instance; one has the feeling in
the case of contemporary European works that a new musical
territory is no sooner discovered than it begins to be "adminis-
tered" rather as the French administered Algeria by making it
into a département *of France, with* lycées *and everything else.*
Thus, an unprejudiced ear would very soon be able, for exam-
ple, to tell without prior knowledge that Pli selon pli *could not*
possibly be the work of an American composer, just as it could
tell without prior knowledge of authorship that your Piano
Concerto could not possibly be the work of a European . . .

There are in Europe canons of taste and quality of thought,
which may be accepted or broken, but which exist more or less
as benchmarks by which a composer orients himself in any
event. Thus nowadays, for example, one will find European
works containing deliberate passages of "bad taste." I don't
think, on the other hand, that Ives ever thought he was writing
music that had moments of bad taste in it—I think he was writ-
ing the music that interested him, reflecting many sides of his
experience and our society. Yet now Ives is fascinating the Euro-
peans because he has what they think of as more or less delib-
erate "moments of bad taste."

Yet, one has this impression of the "differentness" of Amer-
ican works from European ones, even in cases of American works
that are superficially quite "European" in many respects—works
that are obviously thought out to the last detail and in which no
merely "startling" innovations are found, such as Carl Ruggles's
Sun Treader.

One thing about Ruggles is that he doesn't adhere to
the standards of musical texture that a European would. A great
deal of *Sun Treader*, or *Men and Mountains*, is basically a two-
part texture with not very much filled in, except for octave
doublings. It's a very thin but intense texture, contrapuntally

speaking, so that the music is extremely sophisticated for its time in its use of dissonances but very primitive in its textural layout. This dissociation makes the piece seem un-European and makes it not fit into the general ideas of balance that a European would be likely to bring to his work. Of course, this kind of thing is symptomatic of the free attitude that American composers have often brought to the writing of their music—an interest in trying things that in Europe would be considered dangerously out of line with proven esthetic standards. American composers have felt freer to do this, partly because they have not been able to write for a ready-made audience for new music in the way Europeans have been. In a way, American works have been of necessity "private works," given that there has not been a situation in which our composers could believe that what they wrote would be accepted as "American culture" by a society that was depending on their work to constantly feed it with new images of its life. Even Whitman, who thought that he *was* American culture personified, was hardly appreciated in his day, and it was only long after he was dead and began to be recognized as a great poet that he had any influence on the thought of the country. I don't think, on the contrary, that European artists feel this way; I think they feel they're going to have an immediate effect on the country in which they live, and that they're important cultural symbols, something to influence their own society and to be exported as representatives of, say, Germany or France to the rest of the world; and, as a result of this, European artists have to fit into certain cultural standards and canons that their country demands. We in America are free because our culture doesn't make this kind of demand on us. We are left as individuals to float in a kind of cultural limbo.

It's often been said that in practically all the different artistic fields, the greatest artists have almost always stood in a kind of "prophetic" relation to their culture. In America, it's as if the serious composer, of whatever degree of talent and accomplishment, finds himself willy-nilly in such a position . . .

Yes, it's obvious that, for example, while many of the very best works of Beethoven, Brahms, and Wagner went ignored until very late in their composers' lives, and often even then were not recognized for some time, there were simultaneously serious composers at work whose pieces were very popular from the outset with the public of the time. In America, on the contrary, even the most "popular" serious American composers were and are hardly played at all by comparison with the classics and are not very important to our society.

There are many American composers much younger than myself who are aware of this situation and are trying to overcome it by relating their music to the theater. This is because the theater can offer the hope of a less problematic communication with the audience, considering that it deals with materials —words and visual images—that are easier for the public to grasp than purely musical images, which require a more concentrated attention in order to be taken in. Some young composers see the theater as a way of escaping this limbo situation.

On the other hand it's also very difficult to imagine that composers like Schubert or Wolf could exist today in the kind of absolute obscurity that covered their activities during their lifetimes, because now there are so many fellowships and commissions floating around, which are rotated so that almost every possible composer gets one of them once. But the very same system that today, at least in America, seems to preclude *absolute* obscurity, also prevents any very considerable recognition of merit, because everyone gets commissioned once or twice and played once or twice, while few are commissioned or played much more than this. Because those who make choices of this sort seem to have the habit of distributing to as many different composers as possible the limited number of commissions and performances, composers and works recognized by the profession to have quality are brushed aside. This pattern accounts for the atmosphere of discouragement that surrounds so much well-intentioned effort, and does not stimulate anyone to do his best.

To turn for a moment to the directly musical side of this matter, how would you describe the evolution of your own conception of the kind of music you wanted to write in relation

to the evolution of the practical social situation you found your-
self in, particularly after 1944? Especially, would you say that
your awareness of this practical social situation seriously affected
your thinking about your own music, "taken in itself?"

Well, I worked up to one crucial experience, my First String
Quartet, written around 1950, in which I decided for once to
write a work very interesting to myself, and to say to hell with
the public and with the performers too. I wanted to write a
work that carried out completely the various ideas I had at that
time about the form of music, about texture and harmony—about
everything. This work became very much admired, which was
quite unexpected because I really didn't think anybody would
ever understand it at all, and also I didn't think it could even be
played. Now obviously I didn't write it deliberately "so that it
would be unplayable"; I wrote it always with the idea of practical
performance in mind, but from my experience it was beyond
any practical performance that I had ever aimed at before. It was
very much more difficult than anything that I had ever written
and more difficult than almost any work I'd ever heard at that
time. The only work that seemed perhaps harder was Alban
Berg's *Lyric Suite*, which has certain relations with my quartet
—and maybe some of the Bartók quartets—but on the whole
it was considered, at the time, about as difficult as anything that
had been written, even though it is far less demanding than
many works written since.

In any case I decided to do this, and then to my surprise
it won the prize at Liège, and wherever it was played it im-
pressed musical people. When it was played at a festival in
Rome in 1953, for instance, musicians like Dallapiccola and
Petrassi came up to me spontaneously and said how interested
they were. Now, it's also true that there was another side to this
—when it was first played, at McMillin Theater at one of the
regular subscription concerts given then by Columbia University,
I remember that one of the professors got up at the end and said
loudly, "The man who wrote that must be on the faculty here
or it would never have been played." Thus, at the same time
that I had acclaim from musicians, I had violent reactions from

people who just hated the piece. It's very long, and for those who can't make anything out of it, it must be unbelievably tiresome. But it was this work that really set the guidelines of what I wanted to do, and from that point on I decided that I was a composer with a training that had given me the idea of what a public could be, and had taught me to listen to the music I heard in my head the way a possible public might listen to it if it were played in a live situation. This was exactly my idea of what a composer's training really is, or certainly should be in every case. Of course it might not be the public existing at the present time—but if a composer's training is any good, he has the ability to hear his music as another person would hear it. So from that point on I decided that I would just write whatever interested me, whatever expressed the conceptions and feelings that I had, without concern for an existing public.

Now I'm aware that these attitudes can lead to "disastrous'" results, that you can have terribly angry people and terribly angry performers on your hands—and I have. I'm aware of this when I write my pieces; but I've decided that the fun of composing, living as I do in America, where getting recognition is a career in itself and one which I don't care much about, is to write pieces that interest me very much. I don't expect them to be very successful when they're played, but I've had a lot of pleasure and interest in writing them, and in a way they've kept me alive and interested in life, and this helps.

Did you find that what you thought of, purely abstractly, as the horizon of what was possible in or as music expanded as a consequence of thinking it wasn't very important to worry about making everything simple enough for people to grasp on the first hearing?

Oh yes. For instance, I became very interested in the speed of presentation in my music, how rapid and dense it might be, and so on. I began to think about all sorts of different processes and ways of making music hang together which I would probably not otherwise have brought into conscious focus and made into a primary field of thought and musical action. I must say that the one issue that I am, and have been, very concerned with, unlike most of my colleagues since the war, is making the flow of music be the most important thing; the "now" of any given point to me is only as significant as how it came to be "now" and what happens afterward. Therefore to me composing consists in dealing with the flow of music rather than with particular instants of sound, which is why I've never been so very interested in remarkable sounds or effects of any kind for themselves alone, because they seem to evoke a very elementary past or future. On the contrary, I'm very interested in expressing myself by manipulating many kinds of relationships of past and future, because it seems to me that this is the interesting thing in music. Music is the only world in which you can really manipulate the flow of time in a rather free way. For whereas a painter is dealing with a flat, static surface, the musician is working with a constantly flowing stream of sound—so that how you make the stream flow and what obstacles you put in to stop it from flowing or to modify the flow, and so on, become fundamental, and this is what I'm trying to deal with. It's rather hard to do because we're not accustomed to thinking of a temporal succession in one big operation; but I've been trying to train myself over the years really to deal with this particular thing, so that the chords and harmony and motives—or other momentary details—are all subsidiary to the basic concern with the flow of the music itself.

Of course what I'm talking about here does not, as I say, seem to be the concern of most composers today, who generally have the most primitive and obvious way of dealing with time; they do a little bit of something that repeats itself over and over again and then a bit of something else, a pattern that remains most unimaginative no matter how strange the pieces sound. Their only concern is with block-like, terribly simplified structures of time—and this I find distressing.

Parenthetically one might observe that in your music something resurfaces which was for some time very important in Western music but which went underground to a great extent after Wagner—that is the durchkomponieren *idea, as opposed to the notion of short, closed forms, or pieces made up of a block-like succession of these. Except for certain things in Mahler and Sibelius, and in Berg and Schoenberg, there's been a tendency to shy away from organizing whole large worlds of things under one roof, so to speak . . .*

Yes, this is so in a way. Of course, opera composers, of whom there have been so few of high quality in the twentieth century, naturally have the stage and the text to carry them directly into this very field of thought. But it's true that especially since World War II there's been a steady decline of interest in this dimension—to me the overriding dimension of music—such that music has become gradually very much more simplified and simple-minded, for no matter how complicated even serialized structures are, the basic idea and movement is terribly simple, and not merely simple but, to my mind, basically uninteresting because they aren't doing the one thing music can do, which is to "go," to move. Instead, you have static chunks of repetitive design. I find this only one very small and not-too-interesting possibility. We had so much of that with *The Rite of Spring* and the period around it. In fact, I think Stravinsky himself stated later that he gradually lost interest in this way of composing and soon started to develop more interesting continuities, such as those of the *Symphony in Three Movements* and many other later works.

Before going on to deal at length with the directly esthetic and technical questions of contemporary music generally, it might be appropriate to inquire at this point into the circumstances of your own personal development, in the periods both preceding and following your decision to become a composer—beginning particularly with the matter of your own early contact with and interest in serious music.

Well, despite the fact that neither of my parents was particularly musical, they did have a player-piano and decided, when I was in the third or fourth grade, that I should take piano lessons. As a result of this I began to have to learn Chopin and practice scales and the rest of it, all of which I just hated for a very long time. Only when I went to high school did I really begin to take an interest in music—thanks to the fact that I came in contact then with people who were especially interested in contemporary music.

Among these people were Eugene O'Neill, Jr. (son of the playwright) and Clifton Furness, who taught music at the Horace Mann School in New York and knew Charles Ives. Together we went to a great many modern music concerts (this was during the 1920s) and went to visit Ives quite a number of times, when he lived near Gramercy Park (at 120 East Twenty-second Street). In this way I got to know Ives well enough so that he used to invite me to join him in his box at some of the Saturday-afternoon Boston Symphony concerts in Carnegie Hall. In fact, John Kirkpatrick, who is the literary executor of the Ives papers, recently found a letter that I had written to Ives as a high-school student, telling how much I liked his music and thanking him for something or other—and, from what Mr. Kirkpatrick tells me, Ives wrote comments about me in his diary, which I haven't yet read, however.

In any case, going to these concerts with Ives and Fur-
ness, I became immediately interested in modern music—up to
that time, I had been quite bored with any kind of music, never
having heard any modern music. I do remember later taking
my father to hear a performance of *The Rite of Spring* and his
saying that "only a madman" could have written anything like
that. Now as I look back on it, though, I see that my parents
were really very patient and must have suffered a great deal,
because by the time I got interested in contemporary music I
could already play the piano somewhat, and thus they had to
sit through my practicing late Scriabin for hours on end, which
I imagine they found hard to bear—though they never said so.

Mentioning Scriabin, I should probably say here that he was
one of the modern composers whose work I came to know at
this early point and was most interested in. I had become familiar
with his works through Katherine Ruth Heyman, a mystic who
knew almost all of the late piano pieces by heart and was very
interested in theosophy and Rudolf Steiner's "anthroposophy"
(I myself read Steiner's works avidly at the time). She had been
a friend of Ezra Pound, whose "Scriptor Ignotus (Ferarra
1715)" in *A Lume spento* is dedicated to her. In addition she
was the author of a small book, *The Relation of Ultramodern
to Archaic Music*, and used to give musical Sunday afternoons
at her loft on Fourteenth Street and Third Avenue, to which
Ives and a number of people including myself would go. These
meetings had been going on for some years by the time I caught
up with them, for Edward Maisel in his book *Charles T. Griffes*
(p. 179) quotes that composer writing about Miss Heyman in
the New York of 1916: "She played me Scriabin's Sonata No.
8 and other small pieces and also gave us interesting informa-
tion about exotic scales." Indeed, she was still proselytizing for
the later Scriabin in the early '20s and had added the "Emerson"
movement of Ives's *Concord Sonata*, Ravel, Cyril Scott, Emer-
son Whithorne, Griffes and the Op. 11 of Schoenberg to her
repertory. Together with this small group of people interested
in advanced music who gathered often at Miss Heyman's, I
went to hear everything that happened in the way of new
music in New York at the time, including most of the first per-
formances of Varèse. I particularly remember the première of

Intégrales, given in the Wanamaker auditorium and conducted by Stokowski in Varèse's presence, as well as meeting Varèse occasionally at a place in Greenwich Village called "Romany Marie's," a sort of café on Sheridan Square. (These were Prohibition years, and Greenwich Village had the same relation to alcohol then as it has to pot now.)

During this whole period of the early twenties, though, I was much more interested in the very advanced music of the time than I was in anything else and thus came to know the music of Ruggles and Ives, particularly, and Bartók and Stravinsky and the three Viennese—all the new music that was being done in New York in this, a very active period.

Now, I should also mention that I came to know a fair amount about non-Western music and cultures through people I happened to be acquainted with. One of these was Laura Williams, an exponent of Middle Eastern music, at whose house near Douar-Chott in Tunisia I once spent a summer writing down Arabic music played by various musicians whom the Baron Rodolphe d'Erlanger (who was preparing his monumental work on *La Musique arabe,* containing translations of early Arab music theorists, a history of Arabic music, and a volume of recent music in Western notation) invited to his house nearby. That summer he was trying to find musicians who knew the "classic" Arabic style, which was rapidly disappearing under the influence of phonograph records and radio programs that played the latest Western popular music, particularly the Charleston (a dance rhythm close and easily assimilable to Berber music). Then, too, a schoolmate of mine, John Bitter, the son of Karl Bitter (who did the figure atop the fountain in front of the Plaza Hotel), introduced me to Ratan Devi, who specialized in performing and singing East Indian music, some of which I came to know quite well, and to Carlos Salzedo, the avant-garde harpist and composer, with whom Bitter's sister was studying.

At the same time, through the composer Colin McPhee, also a friend, I came to know recordings of Balinese music, and much later was asked to read the manuscript of the big book on the subject which he spent so many years writing.

Then, too, I used to frequent the Roerich Museum at the time before it moved from a Riverside Drive mansion around

105th Street to its present location in the specially-built apartment house at 103rd Street and Riverside. The primitivistic paintings of Roerich (who had earlier provided the sets for the first production of *The Rite of Spring*) with their mystic evocations of Tibet, impressed me very much.

I also went to the Chinese opera in New York's Chinatown and to the performances of the Chinese opera given at the time by Mei Lan-fang's company on a visit to the United States.

Like many at the time, I was very much attracted to exotic music and art and to the experiments in what is now called mixed media. A stage performance of Walt Whitman's *Salut au monde*, with a background of wondrous colored, moving shapes produced by Thomas Wilfred's Clavilux, a color-organ, and with music by (I think) Charles Griffes, left a great impression on me.

The mid-Twenties in New York were very exciting years, and much new music, theater, and art was to be encountered everywhere, even including examples of advanced Russian/Soviet art. Through a schoolmate of mine, Ivan Narodny, in particular, whose father had a small gathering place and theater around East Seventeenth Street, I came in contact with the paintings of David Burliuk and reproductions of the abstract paintings of El Lissitsky and Malevitch that seemed very exciting at the time. I also heard Mayakovsky recite his poetry. As was not unusual for an American then, I was extremely curious about Russia and went to the Eisenstein and Pudovkin films shown at the Labor Temple on Fourteenth Street and Second Avenue—and when the musical wing of the Moscow Art Theater came to give its very "expressionist" *Carmenicita and the Soldier* (a revised version of Bizet) I went many times.

You mentioned earlier that during the twenties there was a good deal of interest in contemporary music among students at the Horace Mann School. Was music taught there as a serious thing?

Yes, it was taught as a serious thing, but there was no question of *modern* music being considered at that time. This was sort of an "underground" affair, not considered acceptable by most people. What was taught was older music, which as I say bored me completely until I grew up. I couldn't stand hearing Beethoven or Bach or Wagner back then. It was only as I started to study music more carefully that I began to like these composers.

What was your first acquaintance with the music of the Second Viennese School?

Well, in 1925 or so I was in Vienna with my father, who used to make frequent business trips to Europe, often taking my mother and me along, and while I was there I bought all the scores of Schoenberg, Berg, and Webern I could find, because a critic I admired—Paul Rosenfeld—said they were very important music. One didn't hear them much in New York at the time, except for *Pierrot lunaire*, which was given three or four times by Greta Torpadie in costume, and sometimes by Archibald MacLeish's wife, Ada, as I remember. In any event, I was very curious about this music and shortly learned the Suite for Piano, Op. 25, of Schoenberg, which had just come out when I arrived in Vienna. I was also particularly intrigued by certain orchestral pieces of Webern and by the Rilke songs, Op. 8, which I had a score of, but could hardly play at the piano, naturally. I also knew Webern's Op. 3 and 4 songs and remember defending them against a savage attack by Theodore Chanler (who himself was a composer, much respected at the time, of elegant, Fauré-like art songs, as well as a critic for the *Boston Herald* or *Transcript*, though I'm no longer sure which).

When you first heard all the very disparate types of advanced music, ranging from Ives and Varèse to Schoenberg and Stravinsky, did it seem to you then that the innovations in the different "dimensions" of music (rhythm, harmony, timbre, etc.) that occurred more or less "separately" in the works of these different composers fitted into some larger pattern of musical evolution, or did you at first see all this as a collection of isolated individual developments?

In my first experience of this music I was primarily struck by its intensity and its power. It was because of hearing it that I decided to become a composer. On the other hand, the clarity with which we hear all these things today is very different from the approach we had when these works were first performed. It was very much harder then to distinguish the many different qualities of this music—one just felt that it all sounded very vital and modern. For instance, I remember making great efforts to analyze some of the later works of Scriabin tonally—not knowing any other way to figure out how they were organized—and coming to no result whatever, although their organization is painfully self-evident to me now. One could see that this music used different kinds of chords, but I was concerned then with making the music fit into the familiar tonal harmony-book patterns with added notes and thus didn't think of considering the chords as "things-in-themselves." This was something that few musicians here had *any* idea about for a very long time. The published "analyses" of modern works that appeared in this early period of modern music (such as Sabanaiev's analysis, in *Der blaue Reiter*, of Scriabin's *Prométhée*—full of errors—or Webern's 1912 article on Schoenberg's music) were not very penetrating or helpful, from a technical point of view, as it seemed to me then, any more than were the discussions of modern harmony in Schoenberg's *Harmonielehre* (1922), Lenormand's *L'Harmonie moderne* (1913), or Hába's *Neue Harmonielehre* (1927). Only in the 1930s did it begin to be clear to me what was being done.

Obviously it was easy even in the twenties to distinguish between Schoenberg, Stravinsky, Bartók and Varèse, but it was very hard to put your finger on what it was that made each so different. For this it was necessary to hear their works many times, to study the scores, to discover not only how much and in what way these composers differed but how much and in what ways they were alike. It's very interesting nowadays, for instance, to hear the works of Varèse and see how he developed his own style out of the early works of Stravinsky. But for many years I had no clearly defined idea of how these things related to each other technically, since few recordings and scores of these works were available. By the 1930s, though, it became clear to me that some composers were very inventive rhythmically, uninventive harmonically and often quite conventional in form, and so on. This discrepancy between the various aspects of musical technique began to bother me. Ultimately it was a sense of this disparateness of dimensions that got me started writing the kind of music I write today.

Was there a specific instance that decided you on composing?

I can't give a date, but certainly *The Rite of Spring* was a very important and meaningful work, as were several of the works of Varèse like *Intégrales* and *Octandre*, and certainly the later works of Scriabin, particularly *Le Poème de l'extase*, *Prométhée*, and the last preludes and sonatas, as well as Ives's *Concord Sonata* and some of his songs. They were all very exciting and beautiful to me, and it was as a result of hearing and thinking about them that I decided to try composing.

Had you already decided on this when you left for Harvard?

Well, I had already tried writing a very "advanced" and complicated piano sonata, as well as some simpler settings of Joyce's *Chamber Music*, which I showed to Charles Ives at the time. He encouraged me to go on and become a composer, which I very much wanted to do, though for a long time I didn't admit this to my parents.

I finally chose to go to Harvard because of its proximity to the Boston Symphony and to all the advanced musical activity that was going on then under Koussevitzky.

When I got there, though, I began to have annoying experiences of enrolling in music courses only to discover that the professors involved couldn't stand one single thing about contemporary music and considered Koussevitzky's modernist activity at the Boston Symphony an outright scandal. Indeed, I found that no one could understand why I wrote what I did when I tried doing harmony exercises, just as I couldn't understand why I should write harmony exercises at all. In fact, I used to discuss with the late Dr. Davison (then a teacher of choral composition and director of the Harvard Glee Club) why one should write choral music that sounded like Mendelssohn and Brahms when I disliked (at the time) the way this sounded. He never gave me an answer that convinced me then. Now I can understand why it might have been worthwhile, but at the time I felt there should be a way of teaching that would help a composer write the kind of music he really wanted to write. It's very much harder for me now, as a sometime teacher, to be sure what sort of pedagogy would accomplish this. Certainly I would have been glad if somebody at Harvard had explained to me what went on in the music of Stravinsky, Bartók, and Schoenberg, and had tried somehow to develop in me the sense of harmony and counterpoint that these composers had, without going through all that traditional stuff, which I didn't like. But this was the order of the day, and finally I got very angry and decided not to study music as an undergraduate. I met other people, like Ralph Kirkpatrick, who also decided that the music department was not for them. In fact, it seemed that everybody who was really interested in music at Harvard went temporarily into other fields—Ralph into painting, and I into English literature—while those who concentrated in music seemed mostly destined to be church organists.

In the end, however, I took my M.A. in music at Harvard, studying with Holst, who suddenly appeared as an exchange professor. Up to that time, from 1926 to 1931, the only person on the faculty really interested in modern music was Walter Piston, who was very sympathetic, having just come back in 1928 from studying with Nadia Boulanger. Of course, while I was there (Ives wrote a letter of recommendation to one of the deans for me to enter as a freshman) * many intellectual influences were very important to me and have remained so through-

---

* Ives's letter to Harvard Dean in *re* Elliott Carter (1926):

"Carter strikes me as rather an exceptional boy. He has an instinctive interest in literature and especially music, that is somewhat unusual. He writes well—an essay in his school paper—"Symbolism in Art" shows an interesting mind. I don't know him intimately, but his teacher in Horace Mann School, Mr. Clifton J. Furness, and a friend of mine always speaks well of him—that he's a boy of good character and does well in his studies. I am sure his reliability, industry and sense of honor are what they should be— also his sense of humor which you do not ask me about." (By permission of John Kirkpatrick.)

out my life. The detailed study of English literature, which in those days stopped with Tennyson but which I supplemented by reading William Carlos Williams, Marianne Moore, T. S. Eliot, Hopkins, Cummings, Joyce, Lawrence, Stein, and others, gave me a very strong sense of the quality and mentality of different historical periods. Aside from the study of German and Greek, both of which have at recurrent periods been picked up and "refreshed," the influence of Irving Babbitt and the "New Humanism" played an important role in a reconsideration of the situation of the modern art of the earlier part of the century. His condemnation of "mixed media" in *The New Laokoon* and of many other excesses of the moderns left a sense of certain limits beyond which art could not go without destroying itself and becoming meaningless. On the other hand, the books and the remarkable humorous urbanity, coupled with extraordinary intellectual penetration, of the lectures of Alfred North Whitehead left a lasting impression and made the "modern" much more comprehensible. *Process and Reality* came out while I was a student, and what I could and can understand of it, along with *Science and the Modern World, Adventures of Ideas,* and his other works, with their stress on organic patterns, have molded my thinking—not only about music. Then there were fellow students like the remarkable Jim Agee, Lincoln Kirstein, Harry Levin, and others deeply interested in modern writing, art, and the film.

Around the Boston area, too, were a number of composers of the previous era, one of whom, Henry F. Gilbert, I used to visit often at his run-down but hospitable house on Ellery Street, Cambridge. The easygoing bohemianism of his family and himself, with his downright American humor, was a great relief after the tensions of Harvard. The Gilberts lived, as I suppose they always had, in what seemed the most reduced of circumstances, even though Gilbert's ballet *Dance in Place Congo* had had a great success at the Metropolitan Opera. I met, too, others more sedate and stoic about their neglect: the witty Edward B. Hill, Arthur Foote, and Charles Martin Loeffler—all very skilled in the turn-of-the-century style, which did not interest me at all then.

Besides all this, I should mention that during a few years of my sojourn at Harvard, there were some very interesting more or less contemporary musical events, over and beyond what was going on at the Boston Symphony. For one thing, the Chicago Opera came a number of times to give its superb performance of *Pelléas et Mélisande* with Mary Garden, who even in those years could project the delicate inflections of her part unforgettably. The "Oh! . . . pourquoi partez-vous?" at the end of the first act, with its rise from G♮ to G♯ on "vous," and the change of harmony that accompanies it, still evoke for me the curious uncertain melancholy (perhaps just the boredom of that old gloomy Maeterlinckian dungeon) that was so characteristic of her extraordinary musical and dramatic performance. Her company also used to give Honegger's *Judith*, which interested me a great deal at the time. Another benefit, as far as I'm concerned, was Alfredo Casella, who conducted the Boston Pops for several years and managed to sandwich large amounts of new music in between old favorites. He was very active during his short spring stays in Boston, and we heard many interesting works, particularly of the French and Italian schools and especially his own. In reading recently his autobiography, *I Segreti della giara*, which I found in a remainder bookstore in Rome, I discovered that this man who spent so much effort conducting new music everywhere had great difficulty in having his own music performed in Italy at that time. We in Boston then knew it better than did the public of Rome, where he lived.

You mention your continuing "distaste" for old music—what was it that finally got you to like it?

Well, later on at Harvard I sang as a hoarse tenor in a Bach cantata club as well as in the Harvard Glee Club. This experience, as well as going to hear the Boston Symphony two or three times a week for six years, and having access to the vast music library of Harvard, which allowed me to study the scores, made older music much more meaningful to me. Then too, when I came to study with Nadia Boulanger, she led her students through practically all the Bach cantatas during the three years I was in Paris. Each week we'd read through two or three of them, sometimes with orchestra and professional singers like Hugues Cuénod, and take turns playing the figured bass and singing recitatifs. Since then the Bach cantatas have remained a kind of "central musical experience" of old music for me. (I remember around that time having a quarrel with Katherine Anne Porter, whom I met at a Thanksgiving dinner at Sylvia Beach's, about the abstractness of Bach. The idea that Bach could have any literary or pictorial intent in his work angered her so much that together through our argument we managed to spoil the whole party.)

What was it that led you to go to Paris to study with Nadia Boulanger after finishing at Harvard?

It had to do with the fact that I'd known French all my life and was then a great Francophile, as I am *not* now. Too, Walter Piston and Aaron Copland, both of whom I admired, had studied with her, and so this seemed the reasonable thing to do at the time. In retrospect, I only wish I had more contact with German culture then. But everything conspired against this. At the time of my decision (1932), big pro-Hitler rallies were taking place that were to lead to Hitler's usurpation, the Reichstag fire and trial at the beginning of 1933. Germany already seemed too involved in distracting social and political problems for a young liberal to study there to become a musician.

Perhaps, too, my decision to study in France was due to many less important reasons. During the First World War, I had absorbed, as any American boy might—especially one living in a Francophile family—a considerable dislike of Germans. In fact, shortly after that war, at the beginning of the twenties, my father took me on a tour of the still horrifying battlefields of Metz, Reims, and Verdun—deserted, chalky, ruined fields where only a few scraggly weeds would grow among rusty barbed wire, and still strewn terribly with human vestiges. This was never to be forgotten, nor was a visit to Berlin and Frankfurt during the devaluation of the German mark, once worth four to a dollar but during that time dropping from ten thousand to several million to the dollar, with prices for Germans rising accordingly, wiping out savings, earnings, the buying power of the whole

nation and reducing it to disastrous poverty in a few short
months. Evidences of this were obvious everywhere. Streets
and stores were empty; waiters snatched uneaten food off plates
before their hungry colleagues could; ordinary people would
stop the foreigner on the street and try to sell him some personal
belonging for contraband U.S. currency. Memories of this heart-
rending catastrophe followed me through my Harvard years,
during which I became very much interested in things German,
and they even colored a few charming summers spent in Munich
with friends, trying vainly to improve my German, following
the Mozart, Wagner, and Strauss festivals (at which Strauss him-
self sometimes conducted), and sailing on the treacherous Starn-
bergersee. I could hardly have foreseen the new holocaust that
was being prepared, especially since young Germans I met were
as pacifist as I.

By the early thirties, however, newsreels began to reveal
the unexpected effectiveness of Hitler's frenzied demagoguery,
and many began to boycott Germany as they had Mussolini's
Italy. Both countries, by that time, had lost their progressive ar-
tistic impetus, which made Paris seem the more important as a
center for new artistic work.

*How would you say your thinking about music was affected
by your studies with Nadia Boulanger?*

The things that were most remarkable and wonderful about
her were her extreme concern for the material of music and
her acute awareness of its many phases and possibilities. I must say
that, though I had taken harmony and counterpoint at Harvard
and thought I knew all about these subjects, nevertheless, when
Nadia Boulanger put me back on tonic and dominant chords in
half-notes, I found to my surprise that I learned all kinds of things
I'd never thought of before. Every one of her lessons became
very illuminating, as she would point out how the parts could
have done this or this. It's such a pleasure to me now to hear
certain of the simplest progressions in the music of Bach and re-
alize that there could have been many other voice-leadings, and
that the one that has been chosen is especially meaningful coming

as and where it does in a particular work. This awareness is extremely hard to communicate to a student, and I don't know whether I would have been in a position to appreciate it if I'd been doing my harmony for the first time with her. In any case, this was very valuable to me as a student composer, for it brought me a full consciousness of the importance of the very smallest details of a musical work and of the way that these can influence the expressive character of the whole.

Then also, when I was studying with Mlle. Boulanger I began for the first time to get an intellectual grasp of what went on technically in modern works. I was there at a time when Stravinsky, who was of course the contemporary composer she always admired most, had written the *Duo concertant* and *Perséphone*, which we all practically had to memorize, along with the *Symphony of Psalms*. The way she illuminated the details of these works was just extraordinary to me, because up to this time I could never see just why a given thing was what it was in a modern piece. All this became clear from the way she explained the Stravinsky works. Now it's also true that at that time she'd come around to disliking the German composers almost entirely, although when Aaron Copland studied with her in the early twenties she was sympathetic to Alban Berg and had the students sing and play over *Wozzeck* in class. That was all past, however, by my time—although more recently, around 1958, I remember going to a rehearsal at the Salle Pleyel in Paris, where Rosbaud and the South West German Radio Orchestra prepared the Five Pieces, Op. 16, of Schoenberg, the Six Pieces, Op. 6, of Webern and the Three Pieces, Op. 6, of Berg, and at which Nadia Boulanger appeared with large scores of each—allowing me to follow while complaining during the Berg that that was the kind of music her students used to write in the twenties. She liked the Webern very much, however, and even remarked that Stravinsky had found a really musical way of writing twelve-tone music.

In spite of such prejudices, which revealed a genuine devotion to the art and an unwillingness to take reputations or other kinds of pressures for granted, she was an invaluable guide to all of music. Her sight-reading of large parts of the *Reihe kleine*

Klavierstücke of Hindemith in counterpoint class bowled us all
over—and one of my very vivid memories is her playing and
singing (with commentary) of the entire orchestral score of a
work she detested—Strauss's *Salome*—in order to answer my
question of what there was of interest in it, since I was going to
hear it for the first time that night at the Paris Opera.

By various tactics, Mlle. Boulanger made all her students
learn to copy music, even counterpoint and harmony exercises,
in India ink and in a fair hand. Also, she pointed out as an ex-
ample the care with which Mahler indicated everything in his
orchestral scores, and a thousand other small and large details
that came to her wide-ranging imaginative mind. At times the
constant display of all kinds of virtuosity was overwhelming,
though never ostentations—such as when she once led me
around Venice, which she was visiting for the first time, having
memorized the *Guide bleu,* giving gondoliers instructions in quite
good Italian and walking into churches she had never seen and
pointing to unusual paintings in dark corners more professionally
(and intelligently) than if she were a guide. It was the despair
of her students, since she was always one step ahead of them,
even of me in English when she was memorizing Shakespeare
sonnets (one a day)—along with all the twelve to fourteen hours
of teaching, nights of conducting, or, in the summer, of leading
small groups of us on walks in the fields around Gargenville at
night discussing everything from Maeterlinck to Machaut. Her
human concern about her students also was very gratefully ac-
cepted by them; for example, when I left she insisted on giving
me a special edition of Pascal's *Pensées,* a work we had talked
about many times while I was a student, and knowing how im-
practical I was, she came over to my little hotel—the Hôtel Stella
on the Rue Monsieur-le-Prince—and in my messy room helped
me pack, insisted on making a list of presents for me to take home
to my family, and then went out and shopped for them, having
called off all her lessons for that day. These constantly unex-
pected acts and remarks, that yet always adhered to a very high
standard of behavior, were unforgettable.*

* These were, of course, those terrible years between 1932 and 1935 in
Paris when the fascist Croix de Feu staged a frightening street fight on the

Then too, Mlle. Boulanger gave a large invited tea party every Wednesday afternoon, after the students had sung through two or three Bach cantatas, at which we would meet Paul Valéry, Raymond Duncan (brother of Isadora), Igor Markévitch (who had previously been Mlle. Boulanger's student), Georges Enesco, and many other figures of the musical, literary, and social world. Mlle. Boulanger herself was widely esteemed in those years, as was evident at the time of her mother's funeral, in which the cortège, which walked from the house on the Rue Ballu to the Église de la Trinité and then to the Cimetière Montmartre, was several blocks long. Her friends and students recently had another reunion that filled the opera house in Monte Carlo, for a celebration of her eightieth birthday given by Prince Rainier (whose *maîtresse de chappelle* she is).

Although she was charming and entertaining sometimes she became formidable. I remember a dinner to which I invited her at La Pérouse, when she sent back the coffee because it was cold and made a scene about how this noble restaurant was not upholding the honor of France. Another time I was chided as conventional for not ordering an iced coffee with panna (whipped cream) before lunch at Florian's in Venice. In her company I was occasionally made uneasy because of my an-

Place de la Concorde during the Stavisky affair, part of which I witnessed. During this time there was a constant stream of refugees from Germany pouring in ever larger numbers into Paris. Soon the police put them anywhere, in warehouses, in old barracks, and even in madhouses, to keep them off the street. A former German musician friend of mine was committed this way and could only be communicated with through a rabbi who visited the *asile* once a week. A few of us worked hard in affairs of this sort and finally obtained his release after about a year. He came out having learned classical Greek.

It was a time of united-front groups aimed to combat fascism, and even though the Moscow trials had embittered many toward Soviet communism, still the Nazi terror was far more immediately uniting than the evident corruption of the Stalinist period in Russia was disrupting.

My political connection with all of this in Paris, though peripheral, was quite separate from my musical life, and while at an earlier time, we had thrilled at seeing the Metropolitan Opera stage filled with waving red flags as the decor for Prokofieff's *Pas d'acier*, now the Soviet Union was looked on with suspicion. Some of us investigated Trotskyism, anarcho-syndicalism, but in the end the real bond was the anti-fascist one. This prevented me from ever visiting Germany after 1928 and Italy from around 1930, except for one short trip to Venice.

tiquated French with all its subjunctives and circumlocutions, which I had learned as a child but which remained of the period when I had learned it and did not cover situations in which a young man necessarily found himself; although I was extremely fluent and of a very large (but literary) vocabulary, it always made a surprising effect on my colleagues, but gave the impression to older French people that I was extraordinarily "bien élevé."

Moreover, as only the French will, Mlle. Boulanger enjoyed identifying the origins of a speaker of French by his usages and pronunciation—not only from which country (in the case of a foreigner) but which *département*, or, of Parisians such as my Harvard French professor, André Morize, just how many years they had been away from the capital. For, as I learned from her amusing mimicry, Frenchmen almost always lose the flavor of their language, the longer they stay away from the heart of their culture—I being thus obliquely reprimanded for my stilted First-World-War style of speaking. Yet this characteristically fine ear for the French of each place and each generation, along with the intense enjoyment of many kinds of highly developed pleasures—wine, food, intensive gardening, *et al.*—coupled with the persistent desire to make even the most troubling situations bearable by compassionate or cynical humor—is one of the impressive things about the French, as is their capacity for extraordinarily clear-headed but passionate love and devotion that lead to great insight—a capacity evident from the time of Joinville's chronicles about Saint Louis and his crusade, right down to the totally absorbing train-ride to Rome described in Michel Butor's *La Modification*. I must say, though, that the widespread *gourmandise* that causes traffic jams by tourists on the *auto-routes* at the starred restaurants for lunch and dinner does not extend itself to music. For in spite of France's musical greatness in the Middle Ages and Renaissance and the appearance of a few masters like Couperin, Berlioz, Bizet, Debussy, and some others, music remains a stepchild. It is not the natural offshoot of French culture, as it is of that of Italy or Germany or Austria. Nevertheless, Mlle. Boulanger valiantly made music in France between the two wars a commanding art. To me her love and enthusiasm for it remain ever present.

Did Nadia Boulanger deal very much with Renaissance music when you were there as a student?

Yes, she did, and so did I, because during those years I was also a member of the chorus of Henri Expert and later conducted a French madrigal chorus myself. As a result I got to know the French madrigal school inside out, and also the English and Italian schools, because at Harvard we'd sung a lot of madrigals. With Mlle. Boulanger we sang a number of Machaut pieces and analyzed them in detail. There were also in Paris occasional concerts of early music—Perotinus, Leoninus, and others—that interested me a great deal.

Parallels are often drawn between the fluid, pretonal polyphonic style and the style of your own recent music . . .

Well, my roommate when I was a graduate student at Harvard, Stephen Tuttle, was a musicologist who later edited the keyboard works of William Byrd for the Musica Britannica scores, and through him I got to know the English madrigals—those of Morley, Weelkes, Byrd, and Gibbons; and the Monteverdi, Marenzio, and Gesualdo works as well.

Did these already seem suggestive to you, from a "technical" point of view, in connection with what you wanted to do as a composer?

Mlle. Boulanger was a very inspiring teacher of counterpoint and made it such a passionate concern that all this older music constantly fed me thoughts and ideas. All the ways you could make the voices cross and combine or sing antithetical lines were things we were involved with in strict counterpoint, which I did for three years with her—up to twelve parts, canons, invertible counterpoint, and double choruses—and found it fascinating.

You mention having liked Scriabin, at one point—a composer who would seem to be at the antipodes from such contrapuntal preoccuaptions. How did you come to feel about this music and other, so to speak, "coloristic" music?

By the time I studied with Mlle. Boulanger, these com-
posers like Scriabin and Debussy had ceased to interest me very
much, and I suppose it was just for this reason. Of course she
admired Fauré a great deal, who seems a kind of middle ground
between the coloristic style and the contrapuntal style, having
Ravel as a successor in some respects. And of course there's
Stravinsky, who in one way doesn't write contrapuntal music
really, but who uses little bits of counterpoint in a very sensi-
tive and remarkable way, I think. But then by this time I had
also come to admire Bartók and Hindemith, who were both very
contrapuntal composers.

*Did you have occasion to meet any of them while you were
in Paris?*

I met Stravinsky, because he used to come to tea at Mlle.
Boulanger's. In fact he once gave a preview of *Perséphone*, with
the tenor René Maison, for the "happy few" at her apartment.
I can still remember vividly the glorious voice (nearly deafening
in the relatively small apartment) that brought to life the part
of Eumolpe, and—what always struck me every time I heard
Stravinsky play the piano—the composer's extraordinary, electric
sense of rhythm and incisiveness of touch that made every note
he played seem a "Stravinsky-note," full of energy, excitement,
and serious intentness.

*After finishing your studies with Nadia Boulanger you re-
turned to America and became, for a while, musical director of
the Ballet Caravan . . .*

Yes, this was one of the many organizations started by Lin-
coln Kirstein, with whom I shared an admiration for the work
of George Balanchine, both of us having seen his works with the
Ballets Russes (*L'Enfant prodigue* and the beautiful *Cotillon*) and
then with his own company, Ballets 1933, in Paris, where the
outstanding *Errante* and *Sept péchés capitaux* were given their
premières. As a result of the fact that Balanchine came to live in
America in 1937, Lincoln Kirstein started the Ballet Caravan as

a troupe of young American dancers, with the idea that this would finally feed into something significant for Balanchine, who was then working here in a rather unimportant way.

In starting the Caravan, Lincoln Kirstein commissioned a number of ballets—one by Paul Bowles, Aaron Copland's *Billy the Kid*, and my own *Pocahontas*. This was my second work to be played publicly, and was written in 1938. The character of the work came from the section of Hart Crane's *The Bridge* in which Pocahontas appears as a sort of "mother-earth" of America. There was an attempt to present this story as seen through the eyes of the English who came as colonialists, and their being saved from destruction at the hands of Nature. At that time the American past was being whitewashed, I suppose in a desperate attempt to make the "melting pot" idea work. I myself had misgivings about the "colonialist" aspect of the subject, particularly as I have some Indian blood of my own, but hoped to make it a parable of cooperation.

Now of course all this happened at a time when the depression was at its worst in America. The musical world here had taken a new turn, toward a kind of populism which became the dominating tone of the entire musical life. The WPA came into the picture at this point and was very helpful for a time, in that it encouraged many composers and played a great deal of American music—though, as I mentioned, this was almost always of a populist nature.

Did you find that audiences generally went along or caught on to this kind of music at the time?

No, audiences just wanted to hear Beethoven and Brahms and Mozart. They were—and still are—in the position I was in as a little boy, when it comes to modern music—they aren't able to distinguish very much about any of these things; they just know new music doesn't sound very much like Brahms, and that's about all, as far as I can see. In fact, I probably should have known better than to try writing works like my First Symphony and *Holiday Overture* in a deliberately restricted idiom— that is, in an effort to produce works that meant something to

me as music and yet might, I hoped, be understandable to the
general musical public I was trying to reach for a short pe-
riod after writing *Pocahontas*. I did this out of a natural desire
to write something many people could presumably grasp and
enjoy easily at a time of social emergency, but I did so without
appreciating just how serious was the audience paralysis engen-
dered by this lack of interest in or familiarity with the new in
any of its artistic forms. Thus I wrote music which escaped the
average listener, despite what seemed to me its directness. Indeed,
I'll never forget taking my *Holiday Overture* to Copland and
going over it with him, only to have even him tell me it was
just another one of those "typical, complicated Carter scores"—
though despite this opinion (which must have been shared by a
number of conductors who saw the work and didn't play it at
the time) Copland was a member of a jury which awarded the
work first prize in a competition shortly thereafter, and in recent
years he has included it in his conducting repertory and has given
by far the best performances the work has received. Indeed, I'd
like to add that, ever since the time of the first performance of
Copland's Piano Concerto with the Boston Symphony in the
late twenties I have been a great admirer of his, and from about
1937 we have been friends; and I have found his development as
a composer consistently exciting and interesting and informed
with a great sense of individual character and a lively imagina-
tion, even in the more trivial works like *Lincoln Portrait* and the
score for *North Star* (in which he managed to make the *Inter-
nationale* somehow Coplandesque).

*Were Copland's own attempts at "comprehensibility" greeted
with any warmth at first, especially considering their subsequent
renown?*

I don't think he had much of a success with *El Salón México*
at first. It was at the time very difficult rhythmically, and Kous-
sevitzky, who had premiered most of Copland's orchestral works,
apparently refused to premiere this one. It was first given in
this country, I think rather inadequately, by Adrian Boult some
years after it was written and only later became successful. How-

ever, the ballet score to *Billy the Kid* (which was premiered on the same program with my *Pocahontas*) was an immediate success, as were *Rodeo* and *Appalachian Spring*. These did not, if I am not mistaken, reach concert audiences until some time later. They were not sought after by symphony orchestras as the latest Shostakovich or Prokofieff symphonies were at the time—although they are more original and imaginative as music. Americans, even Copland, never receive the kind of cultural acclaim reserved for foreigners in our country, although Copland's career, more than anyone else's, served to establish the American composer as one to be taken seriously by the public.

One hears stories of Varèse virtually stopping composing entirely during this period, in despair that people would ever come to like his music, particularly considering the depression circumstances.

It's true that Varèse, whom I used to see occasionally, especially during the time when he was rehearsing my chorus *To Music* with an amateur group, seemed very melancholy during this period, which was turning toward new, more populist artistic aims, thus putting into question the more experimental attitudes of the best artists of his generation. It was easy for me to sympathize with both the old and the new of that time. During my studies and after, so many disastrous human situations resulting from the depression, from the Moscow trials, and from the Nazi-Fascist dictatorships haunted me. It was hard not to feel that very simple human needs were unmet and that the high art we knew seemed cruelly remote from this. Surrounded by so much violence and so much need, one couldn't help wondering whether such a thing as advanced modern music with its élite audience wasn't just beside the point. As Brecht wrote:

Was sind das für Zeiten, wo
Ein Gespräch über Baüme fast ein Verbrechen ist
Weil es ein Schweigen über so vielen Untaten einschliesst! *

* What times are these when
  Talk of trees verges on the criminal,
  Since it includes silence about so many evils?

I'm sure that Varèse felt the same way, and perhaps doubted that his kind of music was worth anything in the light of the problems facing us then, even in the United States. We lived in the midst of a state of affairs that urgently demanded solutions and that made it very hard to find the peace of mind to carry on one's work.

Following a much earlier period in which you appeared to hold strong anti-Expressionist views, your reference in a recent university lecture to musical neoclassicism as "music for a masquerade in a bomb-shelter" must refer to the contrast between this musical style and the political events of the period during which it reached its greatest popularity among composers.

My attitude toward these things has changed a great deal in the course of my life. For one thing, the whole Expressionist point of view had come, at a certain point, to seem as if it were part of the madness that led to Hitler. Indeed, some German expressionists did become Nazis, although many more left Germany, changed their styles, and so on. Gottfried Benn, in whose work I have been interested for years, became an officer in the Wehrmacht until the Nazi authorities caught up with him and made a scandal about his writing, forcing him to retire. Of course certain Expressionist works like those of the Viennese composers, of the painters Kirchner, Nolde, Schmitt-Rottluff, of the writers like Wedekind, Trakl, Döblin, Broch, and Toller have always interested me. In fact, the whole period of the twenties and thirties—coinciding with my student years—were actively involved with the "modern." I was a subscriber to *transition* from its inception to its end, to *The Dial, La Révolution surréaliste,* and *Simplicissimus,* and I read the French, English, and American moderns as well as the Germans avidly. I still have the nine-hundred-page *Dichtung und Dichter der Zeit,* published in 1927 by Albert Soergel, which covers German Expressionist writing with unbelievable thoroughness. I find books on mixed media, like the one by Jean Epstein, very well worn on my shelves, and also Irving Babbitt's fulminations against this in *The New Laokoon* and *Rousseau and Romanticism.* Still, as the Nazi menace grew stronger and the effect of the economic depression, one of its causes, spread, it was not hard to feel that the "excesses" of modern literature were a product of the self-indulgence of idlers unconnected with the catastrophe that was menacing our society. Many people felt—and I certainly was one of them (perhaps not rightly)—that the whole German cult of hypertrophic emotion could have been held responsible for the kind of disaster we were witnessing then in front of our noses (certainly Brecht came to hold this view). This is why, in my opinion, many of us became interested for a time in neoclassicism as a way of "returning to reason" and to a more moderate point of view about expression, as well as to a more accessible vocabulary. After a while, though, before the end of the Second World War, it became clear to me, partly as a result of rereading Freud and others and thinking about psychoanalysis, that we were living in a world where this physical and intellectual violence would always be a problem and that the whole conception of human nature underlying the neoclassic esthetic amounted to a sweeping under the rug of things that, it seemed to me, we had to deal with in a less oblique and resigned way.

When had you first come across Freud?

I had read a number of his works when I was in college. But let me say that all this didn't take on right away the kind of meaning it has since come to have for me. After all, I had my own sort of very early "Expressionist" or avant-garde period, against which I reacted at the time of the depression, and to which I have since returned in a certain sense. I read *Ulysses* practically when it came out and was reading Proust as the later volumes of *À la recherche du temps perdu* were being printed, so this matter of avant-garde art was familiar and was part of a life that revolved around a certain core of ideas, which simply appeared in different lights according to the human and historical experiences I went through at each period. For instance, ever since the beginning I've always liked the music of Schoenberg, Berg and Webern—as much of it as I knew. I was the head of the American ISCM when we gave the first all-

Webern concert in New York—largely at my behest, because
I was especially interested in Webern at that time (about 1952).
I've always been interested in these three composers and have
never had any "reservations" about them. My "anti-Expression-
ist" attitude had to do only with what I myself wished, for a
certain period, to do as a composer. Later I began to see the
Viennese music as more relevant and suggestive in this respect,
though I must say—even though this may sound very strange—
that until quite recently I knew only as much of this music as
I had been able to buy when I was in Vienna in 1925. I now
find to my surprise that some of the things I have done in my
own music have counterparts in some of the Viennese works
with which I remained unfamiliar until a very few years ago.
In fact I found it rather hard to believe my eyes when I came
across that "Monoritmica" in Berg's *Lulu*, which speeds up and
slows down over a whole ten-minute period, something I knew
nothing about when I wrote my Variations for Orchestra. I must
say, though, that in recent years I've become a little fed up with
all this music because I've begun to feel that it is limited in
many ways—though of course no more so than the music of
other great composers, and often less so.

*You mentioned not long ago that you found Webern's music
"charming" but much less interesting than that of Schoenberg
and Berg.*

Yes, this is the way I feel. It seems to me that Webern's
music is so consistently "sensitive," in a "special" vein, that one
can easily have too much of it. In this it's like Fauré—beau-
tiful but very limited. Indeed, I find it extraordinary that it has
become the basis of a "school," except perhaps that certain
people were fascinated by it because it used to be badly played
and seemed intriguingly arcane and chaotic. Actually, it makes
a lot of sense when it's played correctly—rather old-fashioned,
romantic sense—a kind of condensed and refined Bruckner-sense.

*You have mentioned your long-time familiarity with the
work of Ives, Ruggles, and Varèse. How do you presently feel
about these and perhaps other "earlier" American composers,*

*and how have they influenced your thinking about your own
work?*

American composers like Ives, Varèse, and Ruggles have
interested me partly because of the very thing that we talked
about earlier—the fact that they don't fall into the frame of
taste and esthetics we normally associate with European music.
Thus thinking about Ives has been particularly fruitful to me:
about how he calls into question matters of style, coherence,
and even the integrity, the "seriousness" of serious music—and
especially thinking about the whole question of his inclusion of
popular songs and hymns, which has been constantly perplex-
ing.* Sometimes, as in the *Concord Sonata,* his music seems like
the work of an extraordinarily accomplished and skilled com-
poser, particularly the "Emerson" movement, where all the mo-
tivic material is so highly organized and so closely intercon-
nected, as are the harmonic materials. And then there are other
pieces that seem to wipe all this aside and do something else. I
have the impression that Ives must have known very much what
he was doing and thus must have had many different intentions
as a composer—sometimes to write pieces in a high style and at
other times to write sort of angry vaudeville pieces.

Similarly, the whole question of "substance" in music is
posed radically in the works of Varèse, which seem to rest en-
tirely on the sounds of chords and of the instruments that play
them, and on the timbre of percussion. I often wonder how inter-
esting this music will continue to seem years hence, as there
seems to be almost no "substance" to it, in the usual sense, be-
yond these very simple elements. I myself feel that my own
music should somehow have substance, because if it doesn't, I
myself will soon become tired of it, as I do of other people's
music if it doesn't have this. Varèse's music is on the borderline,
and I vary greatly in my estimation of it, although I always end
up returning to it with admiration.

* In one way Mahler is perplexing for the same reason, partly because
some of his works remind one of those old "patriotic symphonies" that were
simply potpourris of national and religious anthems. See my review of the
premiere of the *Concord Sonata, Modern Music* 16, No. 3, pp. 172–76.

I should say that besides these composers I began as far back as 1926 or 1927 to be very much interested in the music of Roger Sessions and, as I mentioned earlier, Aaron Copland. I went to the Sessions-Copland Concerts, given in New York, with great interest, and from the time I heard Copland's *Music for the Theater* and Sessions's First Symphony at the Boston Symphony, and also Sessions's First Piano Sonata, I have followed their music—so different each from the other—with enthusiasm. Both these men, in producing series of exciting and beautiful works, have withstood the terrible process of attrition and destruction that our society visits on its most talented musicians—and each reflects the period of growth of American music in his own strikingly original way.

The development of Sessions's music through his eight symphonies, his opera *Montezuma* (which I heard in Berlin in 1964), and his chamber music, has remained constantly interesting to me for its opulence of sound and imagination. His orchestral works, like those of so many more elaborate moderns, have suffered from inadequate performance and will certainly become an important part of the American repertory when conductors bother to make the effort to find out what is in them. As I pointed out in an article on his Violin Concerto in *The Musical Quarterly*, * Sessions's music has been one long confrontation with the musical materials of our time, first in its late-Romantic and "Impressionist" stage and then in its neoclassic Stravinskyan and Schoenbergian stage. The profound faith in ordered processes of musical thought and expression that go into the making of a work of art as it was conceived by the masters of the eighteenth, nineteenth, and early twentieth centuries, and still is by most of those interested in music, makes Sessions's music very satisfying to follow—full of musical substance and, in the works of his I know best, like the Second and Eighth Symphonies, *Montezuma* (especially the love scene and the finale), and the *Idyll of Theocritus*, rich in expression and idea. Sessions, because of his remarkably wide-ranging culture and ability to describe fine distinctions, has led a successful life of teaching as well as composing and has not had the public exposure that Aaron Copland has

* *The Musical Quarterly*, XLV (July 1959), 375–81.

had. Besides this, his music does not have the immediate appeal for the simple listener of Copland—as is true of Brahms's music when compared with Schubert's. (In making this comparison I recall that Mahler is said to have looked through Brahms's scores and "not found one note of music in them"; certain critics and musicians—though not Copland, I am sure—have made the same gross mistake of judgment in regard to Sessions's works.)

In any case, the public neglect of Sessions would be an outright American scandal if such neglect were not so common, especially by the publics and musicians of the thirties, forties, and fifties. That his wonderful opera *Montezuma* had first to be produced in Berlin before a vociferously anti-American audience is only part of the American process of attrition that drives our composers to despair or sullen stubbornness and discourages their development no matter how talented and promising they may have shown themselves. Sessions has been protected from this (the fate of Varèse, Ruggles, Ives, and many others) by his ability to teach and the devotion of his students and colleagues.

Copland has played the role, as I have mentioned, of a much more public figure, and his music—giving primacy to *character* (like most French and Russian music) over musical thought, while using the latter to reinforce the former—has had a very direct public appeal. Copland has had the opposite problem of development from Sessions—that of dealing with the damage the American publicity machine can easily do to its public figures by constantly drawing attention to irrelevancies and straitjacketing the development of an artist by coarsely typecasting him and then condemning him for not following what is expected of the type. Copland managed to escape from this because his allegiance has really been with his sense of the contemporary and because he has always evolved with the times, despite the obstacles placed in the way of acceptance of the works he has written that transcend the public image concocted for him by publicists.

Both Sessions and Copland have been extraordinarily generous to their younger colleagues, helping them in all sorts of different ways—selflessly organizing modern music societies to perform works of their colleagues (almost never their own), furthering performances elsewhere of young composers they thought worthwhile, and championing them and their works on juries and in print. The development of American music would have been quite different if they had not been so generous with their time and effort.

≪≪≪≪ *III*[*]

*Your own music is marked by an especially close idiomatic or
linguistic tie to the sonorities and techniques of the instruments
and combinations of instruments you've selected for each work.
Is this something that just happens to be the case or is it the
result of a rationalized esthetic decision?*

It's always seemed to me that instruments, in a certain sense,
offer one materials for composition just by virtue of having, as
they always do, built-in "character-structures," so to speak,
which can be suggestive of musical possibilities both on the level
of sonority and on that of actual musical behavior. If one pays
no particular attention to this fact, then one automatically has
in mind some other generalized idea of sound and musical char-
acter, which particular instruments are made to fit after the fact.

* Many of the questions in this section are of a partly technical nature.
These were posed not out of concern for mere technical detail, but primarily as
a means of getting at esthetic issues highly refractory to direct discussion in
words. This refractoriness is a well-known problem in all music, tonal or
"atonal," and can no more be construed to indicate a "lack of poetic substance"
in the music here under discussion than it can in cases where technical discus-
sion is resorted to in order to clarify the poetic thought processes of "standard
repertoire" works. Such technical questions as here follow are of practical
value not only to performers, composers, and music students, but equally
to listeners whose spontaneous esthetic grasp of contemporary music is al-
ready strong enough to lead to a curiosity about "how it is done"—specifi-
cally, as a means of gaining further insight into underlying poetic motiva-
tions. It should be clear, moreover, that "technical questions" in music are
ipso facto esthetic questions (though in recent decades much so-called
technical discussion by certain composers might suggest this was not so),
simply because technical questions deal with the means by which alone a
composer realizes the poetic idea that inspires his work. A purportedly direct
verbal discussion of poetic intentions very soon founders on the fact that a
poetic idea in music requires a *musical* expression, which, if not spontan-
eously self-evident to the listener in its general outline, cannot alternatively
be communicated by words. [*A. E.*]

It's obvious, for example, that Stravinsky and Copland work at the piano when they compose and then transfer, in many cases, the percussive character of pianistically-based ideas to, say, the orchestra, and that their musical conceptions are to a degree independent of their final instrumental incarnation. This was also the case, I understand, with Ravel, and was invariably true of composers in the Renaissance and much of the Baroque. In these periods the musical language was, so to speak, "indifferent" to the possibilities of differentiation of musical character that are latent in any group of instruments. It's really only with the Classical period that a repertoire of kinds of *écriture* related to the sonorities and technical peculiarities of particular instruments arises. This began to be used in a dramatic way by Mozart, particularly in his piano concertos, where often one instrument is made to "imitate" another by playing a passage of a character usually associated with that other instrument—that is, say, the piano soloist will play a distinctly "horn call" type of figure, which the horns will answer, and so on. In this case the sonorous characteristics and behavioral possibilities of the instruments play a role not only in that they suggest varied and distinct kinds of musical materials, but also in that they become dramatic identities that can be played off against each other in many ways and thus actually help create the musical argument itself.

Now in more recent times there have been contrary attitudes on this question—some composers have attempted to reinstitute a kind of "uniform canon" of musical sonority and behavior to which instruments would then be made to conform. This is true of Hindemith and is markedly the case with Webern after his Op. 20. The serialists of more recent vintage have carried this even further. ("L'après-midi d'un vibraphone"—with the *o* pronounced Germanically—has lasted now for over fifteen years.) I myself, however, have been interested in pursuing the possibilities of dramatic contrast and interplay offered by the individual character of instruments and have attempted in all my works, at least since my Piano Sonata, to exploit these possibilities in the most vivid ways I could imagine. Of course one might ask whether there could be such a thing as a "totally idiomatic" piece—whether a piece, or a part in a piece, could be written that would employ *only* those kinds of sonority or gesture "peculiar" to the instrument in question—but naturally this cuts out one dramatic possibility, which is to have an instrument play *against* its nature. And of course in any "dialogue," musical or otherwise, there must be areas of overlap and interchange as well as points of divergence. Thus in my music there is a kind of ongoing dialectic of affirming and contradicting the character of the instruments involved, which nonetheless have an organic relation to the character of the musical ideas and to the formal-dramatic conception of the whole work in each case.

As I said, this kind of thinking begins in my music with the Piano Sonata of 1945, but first takes on special dimension in the Sonata for Cello and Piano I wrote on a commission for Bernard Greenhouse in 1947. In thinking about writing the work, it struck me as interesting *not* to try to "flatten out" or to conceal the great built-in characterological discrepancies between the cello and the piano, as was often done in earlier works of this type, but rather to make this difference of character an explicitly meaningful aspect of the piece. Thus the opening Moderato presents the cello in its warm expressive character, playing a long melody in rather free style, while the piano marks a regular clock-like ticking. This ticking is interrupted in various ways to situate it in a musical context which indicates that the extreme dissociation between the two instruments is neither a matter of randomness nor of indifference, but is to be heard as having an intense, almost fateful character. Then at the end of the final Allegro this idea returns with the roles of the instruments reversed. The musical idea or point is thus inseparable from the instrumental medium out of which it grows. This is generally true of all the works I wrote after the Cello Sonata. For example, the whole range of musical expression, details of shape, phrasing, rhythm, and texture, as well as the large form of my Sonata for Harpsichord, Flute, Oboe and Cello were all determined and grew out of a desire to explore the many colorful possibilities of the modern harpsichord, with the other three instruments serving as a frame to set this off in best relief, and with their "musical behavior" conditioned by this aim.

Considering that a "permanent esthetic conception" of this type would seem to presuppose in each case a thorough technical familiarity with the chosen instruments, it would be interesting to know in some detail how you went about composing the technically very demanding as well as extremely exciting solo part of your recent Piano Concerto—especially in view of the fact that so relatively little "virtuoso" keyboard music of genuine esthetic moment has been written in an advanced post-tonal idiom, and that even Schoenberg's Piano Concerto remains so modest from this point of view.

I should say, first of all, that it perplexes me to find the piano part of Schoenberg's Piano Concerto so "barely" written; after all, he wrote a number of piano pieces that show an original yet idiomatic command of the instrument and are much more advanced in the use of piano technique—the gigue of the Suite, Op. 25, for instance, is really very brilliant and well written for the piano, as are quite a number of the pieces in Op. 23. These suggest that Schoenberg was familiar with the piano's possibilities in a very basic way.

Now, in my case, I *can* play the piano, though not terribly well. I actually played the Schoenberg Suite in public when I was a boy, when it first came out. But I haven't practiced the piano seriously for many years, partly because I am a very nervous public performer; but I am very familiar, naturally, with how you play the instrument, and didn't consult anyone in writing the solo part in the Piano Concerto, the way Brahms did in writing his Violin Concerto. I did talk to Stravinsky about the problem of piano writing, and he said the best way to find things out was simply to practice etudes, which I did—particularly the Brahms *Klavierübungen,* which Jean Casadesus once introduced me to. I found them very entertaining because they have things like three-against-five and so on. So I guess my Piano Concerto comes from these as much as anything. Then too, I studied all the old piano concertos I could find and decided, given the kind of conception that I had in mind, that I had to write an elaborate piano part. This was partly because I wanted to write a comparatively simple orchestral part. Actually, the piano part comes directly out of the technique of the piano part in my Double Concerto, though in the Double Concerto I realized that the piano couldn't be a great thundering force without killing the harpsichord, and thus had to be kept rather light in texture. When it came to the Piano Concerto, though, where the soloist is pitted against the whole orchestra, I realized that I would have to use a chordal style to produce many degrees from very light to very emphatic piano writing.

Considering that the piano is a resonating instrument and that the use of the pedal can have such drastic effects on the harmonic sound of a passage, how did you approach the matter of pedal notation in the Piano Concerto?

Of course, in tonal music you can allow the tonic and dominant chords to interpenetrate, by sustaining the one with the pedal and then sounding the other, and still listeners will hear them as distinct chords, though they're present simultaneously. In post-tonal music, the pedal problem in piano music is more complicated because of the absence of fixed harmonic identities. I only indicated pedaling where I require successive chords to interpenetrate. In general, since a great deal of my music is polyphonic, it's important not to have too much pedal, so you can hear the polyphonic voices. And, of course, in the Piano Concerto the orchestra and concertino often fulfill the role of the pedal—that is, usually something is being sustained by the orchestra so that the piano isn't just left naked. But over and beyond the problem of the pedal, there's a very great problem of notation in keyboard music, such that one never knows quite whether it is clearer to write note-values corresponding exactly to the desired resonance duration, or to let the performer decide on this on the basis of a given notated attack-pattern. I find I notate in one way or the other according to the musical situation.

In keeping with your feelings about the relation between musical language and instrumental media, you have heretofore not had recourse to electronic or other "unusual" sound sources in composing your works. Many composers, on the other hand, have explained their interest in electronic media by reference to the alleged shortcomings and limitations of the usual instrumental groupings, most particularly those of the symphony orchestra. How do you presently feel about the problems and possibilities of orchestral writing?

One has to consider that the symphony orchestra as it is presently constituted reflects in its grouping and composition the textural and timbral earmarks of the kind of music it was historically evolved to play—that is, mainly "harmonic" music. Thus one finds wind instruments grouped always by threes and fours to accommodate the triads and seventh chords of tonal music. Similarly, the families of instruments cover ranges from high to low in each case to permit the ubiquitous octave doublings characteristic of the tonal orchestral style. The large number of string instruments reflects a preoccupation with fat sonorities on the part of composers like Brahms and Strauss, whose music was just about the last, chronologically, to affect the physical makeup of orchestras, and that make-up has been standardized and preserved without change to this day.

Writing post-tonal music for an orchestra of this kind presents a great problem, which might be called the problem of the "tutti"—that is, since octave doublings are excluded or are to be used in a special way in the vast majority of cases (as a result of the modern practice of avoiding the octave as a functional interval), there is a real problem in giving a hundred players something to do simultaneously. The special attitude toward octaves means that one must either double at the unison or else write an extremely thick "divisi" texture, with each instrument doing something totally different from the next one. The only apparent alternative to this is to adopt Stravinsky's recent program of the "giant chamber orchestra" and have only a very few instruments play at once, with the musical line passing from one little group to another constantly throughout the piece. To me this solution seems to beg the problem, as far as my own music is concerned, because I feel one might as well just have a chamber orchestra and not play around with color for the sake of color; if one has a hundred players together in one room, they should be given something to do simultaneously, at least part of the time. That is, once again, I feel that the musical language or thought ought in each case to grow out of the possibilities of the instruments or groupings of instruments at hand, and in the case of the orchestra one of the possibilities— the distinguishing possibility—is that of simultaneous playing. Yet how to deal with this, even "theoretically," is a problem today.

My new Concerto for Orchestra divides the orchestra up into packs of concertini, many of which sound different musical character-continuities at the same time. And since, in keeping with the consideration of orchestral density, the work is all based on five- and seven-note vertical combinations, I had to think of musical ideas that, say, five double basses could play and that would sound well without being blotted out by or blotting out what the other groups of instruments are doing at the same time. This is one of the most acute problems in contemporary orches-tral music: the problem of instrumental balance. One can never be terribly sure just how clearly everything will sound when one is dealing with previously untried textural combinations. The instruments have such different dynamic weights and vary so much in strength according to register that one always runs risks of having a perfectly clear musical idea come out sounding like muck because of the imponderables of orchestral chemistry, which can often be worked out only by trial and error—espe-cially the more unconventional the textural idea.

From a "purely compositional" point of view, the best thing would be to be able to select the exact instrumental combination one requires for each composition, rather than be saddled with a "standard" ensemble of a hundred or so players. We all may fondly recall the days before World War I when Schoenberg could write a piece like *Die Jakobsleiter* or the *Orchestral Songs*, Op. 22, calling for ten horns or six clarinets, exactly correspond-ing to his musical requirements. Nowadays the economics of the orchestral situation make prohibitively expensive the addition and subtraction of large numbers of players from the "standard" grouping to accommodate the possible imaginative orchestral

conceptions of new pieces—or so we are told. And now, even
with the standard ensemble, once one has produced a piece one
is faced with the terrible restriction of rehearsal time and the
insecurity or hostility of conductors who just want to get it
over with and go on to the Strauss piece that will get them im-
mediate applause. Without the help of a serious conductor, the
musicians have no idea how to balance with each other in a
musical texture unlike that of the tonal works they are trained
to play, and thus they cannot give a recognizable or convincing
performance of a new piece. I don't know how many countless
modern orchestral works have been damned on the basis of in-
competent, insufficiently rehearsed performances.

In addition to these circumstantial problems, there is the
built-in problem of players' reflexes in large instrumental group-
ings, which requires the composer—at least a more advanced one
—to simplify his rhythmic vocabulary to a degree, though this
can be compensated by the density factor not available in cham-
ber music.

I should say, finally, that in writing my new orchestra piece
I was interested in trying to find new "central" sound-bodies
from which musical ideas grow and to which they return; that
is, it's obvious in all orchestral music before Mahler that the
string instruments are the "basic sound" and that the brass and
woodwinds, to say nothing of the percussion, have a dependent,
superstructural role in the continuity, from the point of view of
timbre and character. With Mahler this sound-scheme is reversed
for the first time, and the wind instruments come to the fore,
with the strings playing often a secondary and sometimes an
equal role. In my new piece, I have tried all kinds of things in
this domain in order to bring the orchestra into a new light, one
that reflects the multiple simultaneous layers of continuity on
which the work is based.

*Since you will shortly be working on a third string quartet,
it would be of interest to know how you feel about this medium,
in view of the stringent limitations of harmonic density and
timbral variety it automatically imposes.*

Well, as far as color goes, I still believe that the real interest
of music lies in its organization, and therefore the lack of variety

of color in the string-quartet combination is not terribly disturbing to me. In fact, in neither of my previous quartets have I used the "eccentric" techniques of string writing—I've never used *col legno*, tapping on the wood, or playing behind the bridge; I might in the next one, but I haven't so far. And in the Second Quartet the only thing that's "novel" is that there's one instrument that plays unusual kinds of pizzicati every once in a while. To me the real problem, and the interesting one, is to deal with the medium as it is and get something out of it that's expressive and vivid to me. I don't believe in novelty of sound for its own sake; that's always the easiest thing to bring off and loses its interest very quickly.

Had the string-quartet medium interested you long before you wrote your First String Quartet?

I had written two other partially completed quartets before that. I don't remember just why in particular I started writing what became my First Quartet, but I soon discovered, once the piece was written and began to be played, that the standards of ensemble playing in quartets and the general sensitivity and imaginativeness of quartet players—especially their willingness to try new things and to practice them well on their own—are very far above the average one encounters among performing ensemble musicians in general. This is very encouraging to a composer in the context of the acute performance problems he runs up against as a matter of course nowadays.

You've mentioned elsewhere a progressive change in your music over the past ten years away from more or less strictly linear conceptions to a more "textural" and discontinuous écriture. The string-quartet medium would seem the linear medium par excellence . . .

Actually, I've found that quartet players can do almost anything you could imagine. And while there has been an evolution in my music, still I have never used certain less common ways of playing, for the simple reason that the more one gets away from the chromatic scale and distinct pitches, the harder

it becomes to make any kind of interesting imaginative tem-
poral pattern—"substance," if you like—which as far as I'm
concerned is the basic issue. Thus I find I am rapidly bored with
music that is entirely "textural" in its construction, like a lot of
recent Stockhausen and much of the new Polish music. The
"textural" effect by itself ceases to be surprising after the first
hearing, because it is immediately clear that it does not con-
tribute to any but a very primitive and simple-minded point-to-
point continuity of sound-moments, whose interrelations offer
no food for thought after the fact, nor indeed any basis for the
kind of "suspense" that results from the listener's formal-
dramatic expectations about the future course of the piece as it
is going on. Of course, in a frantic effort to overcome the te-
dium of so much of this textural and coloristic music, composers
have been driven to "collage" techniques, claimed to be de-
rived from those of painters. The cutups and repastings of frag-
ments of the musical classics (sometimes upside down) that
Italian Dadaists used to do as jokes are now a respectable part
of musical technique for some. The actual collage-type pieces
of Stravinsky, like the *Symphonies of Wind Instruments*, are,
of course, much closer to most painters' collages, like those of
Picasso, Matisse, and Schwitters, since the over-all concept of
the work dominates and assimilates the heterogeneous materials,
making them produce one homogeneous impression.

Furthermore, unless it is very good theatre (which is rare),
music that is not, so to speak, textural in this way, but that aims
at a kind of theatrical *musique concrète*, often bores me be-
cause of its poverty of ideas. One cannot be *musically* inter-
ested by people hitting on a brake-drum or on the floor, or
smacking each other on the face—this is hardly interesting as
sound and is "surprising" only in that you don't expect it in
the surroundings of a concert hall. Now, God knows I don't
expect much in the surroundings of a concert hall—I just go
and hope I'm going to hear some good music. I'm not interested
in the *decorum* of the place, which is all that is really in ques-
tion in this kind of music. We used to hear a lot about people
going to concerts primarily for "social" reasons, and I think
the same is true—in "reverse" fashion—of these people who
go to hear music played on barbecue trays and glasses of water:

they are merely a more up-to-date version of those socially-motivated subscribers to the Boston Symphony.

In this connection it would be interesting to know how you feel about your own relation to what is called "musical tradition" —a term that has been so often bandied about in an attemptedly pejorative manner by certain of the more pompously self-anointed popes of "musical modernity."

It seems to me that tradition provides not only a way of carrying on but also a way of turning away. People not basically aware of the tradition by which they are automatically conditioned are always the most acutely traditional—in just the pejorative sense they are so painfully anxious to avoid. I realize that what I am trying to do in music always remains in a "restricted frame," in that I try to write music that will appeal to an intelligent listener's ear and will be a strong enough expression so that the listener will be drawn to hear and grasp this music when it is presented by a performer who finds it gratifying enough to play effectively. It may take many years for the listener to be convinced, but I believe that my training and experience as a composer enable me to prejudge a possible future listener. In my opinion, the idea of writing a piece of music that no listener would ever be able to understand or enjoy is utterly incomprehensible. I sometimes hear others' music that I think to be of this sort, but later come to understand it; in other cases I continue to be mystified even after many hearings. And finally in these cases I begin to wonder what kind of composer is behind this, since there seems to be a willful desire to be unintelligible forever. And though this is to some degree understandable in terms of the "literary" movements that surround us, I find it utterly alien to my own conception of the nature and purpose of music, whether one wants to call this purpose traditional or something else.

Over and beyond this, I'd like to point out that, in a somewhat different direction (though one often raised in challenge to so-called traditional notions of music), the matter of improvisation brings up a whole swarm of problems, including the idea that performing a score is "limiting to the individuality of the performer." This notion was clearly expressed by William God-

win in 1793.* Of course this amiable paleo-anarchist believed
men were "perfectible," that conversation with woman was more
rewarding than sex, which he considered "a very trivial object."
Carrying his kind of thought about musical performance one
step further, one could say that it is harmful to be subjected to
being a listener or reader, since such activities make one the
slave of another's thought. In fact, the individual can be con-
sidered a slave of his own bodily needs—so where do you stop,
on the road to "perfectibility"?

From a purely musical point of view, I've always had the
impression of improvisation of the most rewarding kind when
good performers take the trouble to play music that is carefully
written out as if they were "thinking it up" themselves while
they played it—that is, when with much thought and practice
they come to feel the carefully written-out piece as a part of
themselves and of their own experience, which they are com-
municating to others directly from themselves in the moment
of the performance, in an alive way.

On the other hand I've heard endless numbers of so-called
improvisations, especially by mechanically-trained classical music
performers turned avant-garde, which lacked the slightest trace
of aliveness and musical intelligence of any kind, and amounted
to a mere bag of limited clichés these performers had picked up,
rather poorly, from hearing performances of written-out works
in a "modern" style. These clichés were nothing the improviser
had felt out for himself, and were always thrown together in a
meaningless way in the excitement or panic of the public mo-
ment, never growing out of the sustained, spontaneous, and per-
sonal musical invention that is always in play in the improvisa-

* "Everything that is usually understood by the term cooperation is to
some degree evil. . . . We cannot be reduced to clockwork uniformity. . . .
Shall we have concerts of music? The miserable state of mechanism of the
majority of the performers is so conspicuous as to be even at this day a topic
of mortification and ridicule. . . . It may be doubted (hereafter) whether
any musical performer will habitually execute the compositions of others.
. . . All formal repetition of other men's ideas seems to be a scheme for im-
prisoning for so long a time the operations of our own mind. It borders in
this respect upon a breach of sincerity, which requires that we should give
utterance to every useful and valuable idea that occurs to our thoughts." In
his *Enquiry Concerning Political Justice*, London, 1798, Vol. II, pp. 846–47
(facsimile of third edition, Toronto, 1946).

tion of the composer, who then writes down as best he can what he hears so that others can realize it in performance better than he could himself—just as he, as a composer, thinks things up naturally (though with great care and effort of "focusing") better than people whose skills happen to lie most naturally in the area of execution.

You could say that a musical score is written to keep the performer from playing what he already knows and leads him to explore other new ideas and techniques. It is like a map leading a hiker through unknown country to new vistas and new terrain, revealing to him new possibilities of experience that he did not know he could have.

At one time it was thought that a high skill brought freedom with it, the freedom of being able to accomplish certain valued actions with ease. The more the violinist practices, the easier it is for him to play intricate passages with freedom. . . . How would he have known just what such intricate passages might be without their inventors, the composers, who gave him something to work at and express himself with and thus communicate intelligibly with us?

With this matter of intelligibility and communication you raise all the esthetic and, by the same token, all the technical questions of musical composition in the post-tonal era. That so much effort, and what often seems frenzy, have been invested over the past four decades in attempts to rationalize post-tonal language would appear to be evidence of considerable perplexity on the part of many composers in trying to deal with these questions. In writing your own works you have conspicuously avoided fealty to any of the various systems, particularly the serial system, that have purported to provide a rational basis and method for coming to terms with the linguistic problems of post-tonal music.

Specifically what are your feelings about these systems and, perhaps by contrast, what do you yourself see as constituting the necessary basis of a genuine post-tonal "musical rationality"?

To begin with, it seems to me that there is an obvious hierarchy of values in this matter, a hierarchy that has been fatally overlooked by many in their attempts, systematic or otherwise, to come to grips with these problems. As I see it, there is in every case *first* of all a general desire for communication and only secondly a desire for what I call "making musical sense," which begins to employ a sort of rationalized or ordered system, and does so *only* to achieve the desired communication, which must therefore in every case be the prime and ultimate determinant of any musical system pretending to genuine *musical* rationality.

Now in my opinion a great many of the recent systems are not rational at all in this sense, which, as I see it, is the only possible sense the term can have in music. That is, these systems are perfectly fine as abstract schemata of one kind or another, but are often useless for musical purposes, simply because they don't have any particular relation to the composer's desire to communicate feelings and thoughts of many different kinds, which, as I say, are logically prior to the evolution of any system. This lack of relation to the composer's desire to communicate goes together with the fact that these systems lack any relation to the *listener's* psychology of musical hearing. The so-called "system" of tonal harmony was obviously not invented as a mechanically or arithmetically perfect system on paper—it was invented by constant *musical* experiment over many years by composers attempting to communicate something to intelligent listeners. If tonal harmony had been invented in a purely Pythagorean way, it would have been of extremely limited serviceability from any musical point of view, and that's how I feel about the many kinds of serial systems.

What you are talking about has to do with a long historical debate on the nature of order and meaning in works of musical art in particular, one side of which insists on essentially mechanical criteria, the other on what might be called "psychological" or "dramatic" criteria, for lack of better terms . . .

It's obvious that the real order and meaning of music is the one the listener *hears* with his ears. Whatever occult mathematical orders may exist on paper are not necessarily relevant to this in the least. Now it's true that in writing my own works I sometimes try quasi-"geometric" things in order to cut myself off from habitual ways of thinking about particular technical problems and to place myself in, so to speak, new terrain, which forces me to look around and find new kinds of ideas and solutions I might not have thought of otherwise. Nonetheless, if what I come up with by these methods is unsatisfactory from the point of view of what I think is interesting to *hear*, I throw it out without a second thought.

Now in the case of certain types of serialism one is clearly dealing with an essentially visual-mechanical kind of "logic," which does not insure its being audibly perceptible or its conveying any musical meaning through its structure. And it is certainly a question whether the "logic" of a mechanically-ordered system of pitch and durational successions can be made to produce a psychological effect on the listener consistent in detail with the composer's expressive intentions. It thus seems to me that the serial system requires a great deal more manipulation than is often realized if a composer is to write a more or less consistently effective piece. What happens is that the system itself gets to be so intricate that it begins to usurp the attention that should be spent on making musical statements and devising whole continuities of these. On this matter of continuity, serialism gives only the simplest kind of schematic information.

There seems to be a sort of unspoken feeling on the part of a great many recent composers that the only way they have of making their music appear "real" and "rational" in the eyes of contemporary society—and first of all in their own eyes as products of its educational influence—is to make their music conform as far as possible with the prevailing conventions as to what constitutes reality and rationality. That these conventions are mechanistic-technological in essence must be clear to many people by now, and that they are incompatible as such with properly artistic aims is reflected in the refusal of the institutions of (particularly) American society to take seriously anything which, like music, is not convincingly graspable in terms of these conventions.

This may well be the case and might help explain the virulence of this phenomenon in recent times, though the abstract argument on this question has a long history, as you mentioned, and dates back at least to the antithesis between the views of Pythagoras and Aristoxenus.* Nonetheless it is important, from a musico-historical as well as theoretical point of view, to emphasize that the origins of the serial method had little to do with this kind of mechanistic thinking—that is, the twelve-tone method as it was developed by Hauer and Schoenberg was largely concerned with the production of closely related sets of melodic and harmonic materials for use in what remained a traditional melody-and-accompaniment scheme. Furthermore, though this twelve-note method, being treated thematically, bears a marginally audible relationship to the musical qualities of the best pieces in this style, such as Schoenberg's Variations for Orchestra, the most important part, by far, of the musical effect of these works is achieved by other musical means than the serial business, which is all most teachers and students take the trouble to analyze. That is, the functioning elements of the musical rhetoric in these works are not always pitch elements as such, but are more apt to be rhythmic-dynamic or textural elements (in the general sense), or shifts of tessitura, with precise pitch-relations playing a secondary role. Thus the functioning elements remain independent of the serial organization of some of these early twelve-tone works, somewhat after the manner of those old folklore tone-poems that could give a similar treatment to Czech, French, Spanish, or Oriental themes.†

* Aristoxenus criticizes the numerological, Pythagorean school for not being concerned with the function—the power or "dynamic"—of the notes in scales and melodies. *Harmonics*, Book II, 32–33: "The subject of our study is the question: 'In melody of every kind, what are the natural laws [psychological principles] according to which the voice, in ascending, or descending, places the intervals?' For we hold that the voice follows natural laws in its motion, and does not place the intervals at random. . . . For some of [our predecessors] introduced extraneous reasoning and, rejecting the senses as inaccurate, fabricated ['] rational ['] principles, asserting that height and depth of pitch consist in certain numerical ratios and relative rates of vibration—a theory utterly extraneous to the subject matter and quite at variance with the phenomena. . . ." H. S. Macran, *The Harmonics of Aristoxenus*, Oxford, 1902, pp. 123–24.

† However, formal coherence is often achieved by deriving *motives* from the tone-row and its inversions and reversions, the desire for which

Total serialism differs completely from this, because it invades every dimension of the musical rhetoric and predictably produces disastrous results, from any artistic standpoint, in the vast majority of cases. It's as if one were to make a statistical abstract of meteorological data over a certain period and proceed to construct a building on the basis of the figures thus obtained—and then attempt to justify a particularly chaotic jutting of the wall of the building on the grounds that the wind velocity was over 150 miles per hour on February 23, or some such nonsense. This kind of thing may *by chance* occasionally produce an interesting event or texture in music, but the musical interest of this event or texture will be independent of the method by which it was cooked up, just as the vast majority of textures and events concocted by these methods are musically null, though products of equally ingenious number games.

Thus the only thing to be said for total serialism is that, as a method of producing sound patterns that were never heard or thought of before, it has occasionally contributed to the expansion of the composers' available vocabulary. However, the criteria of musical sense, according to which such material can be effectively put to work in an actual piece, have nothing to do with the kind of mechanical thinking and procedure by which this kind of material is often first arrived at. In my opinion many composers have not been sufficiently aware of this.

In view of the fact that the twelve-tone method was not formulated until the early twenties, long after the real "atonal revolution," and further considering what you said about the continuing independence of much of the functional rhetoric of the early serial pieces from the serial method itself, it would be interesting to know how you think composers (like Schoen-

---

motives existed in the composer's mind before he wrote the row, and wrote it in a way that would allow such kinds of motivic coherence. Similarly, the whole concept of symmetrical phrases such as exists in much of Schoenberg's Variations for Orchestra, is *prior* to devising a row which would permit this. The wish to realize such traditional formal patterns must have preceded the choice of the row. In most cases, many of a composer's expressive and formal intentions must exist before the choice of a row, just as they did before the choice of a theme, often affecting this choice very directly. Once made, a whole new group of possibilities arises from the specific notes, naturally.

berg) at the actual turning-point of modern music made sense
of what they were doing without tonal centers to guide them—
which is another way of approaching the question of "rational
linguistic criteria" in post-tonal music.

First of all, these composers evolved their atonal language by
very slow degrees—not all of a sudden, as the impression is often
given by commentary on this question. Furthermore, at *all* times
they composed their music in accordance with the specific type
of musical or expressive *character* that they wished to produce.
In some ways this is a far less mysterious affair than it is often
made to seem, as becomes clear if one takes a close look at cer-
tain of Richard Strauss's works, particularly *Salome* (1905) and
Elektra (1908). Here you find a great many passages that closely
resemble the musical style of the early atonal works of Schoen-
berg and Alban Berg. In fact, I'm sure that, if one were to lift
these passages out of their "tonal" contexts in the actual Strauss
works and play them separately, they would seem surprisingly
"atonal" and "Expressionistic." So in fact this kind of Expression-
istic musical gesture and character crept slowly into the cur-
rent musical vocabulary and was at first compatible, esthetically
and technically, with a tonal framework or style. Thus I don't
think the first atonal composers ever felt "at sea" about any of
this, technically or otherwise. It's perfectly clear that the other
"revolutionaries" like Scriabin and Debussy and Stravinsky ap-
proached emancipated dissonance by similar means—at first ac-
cepting and taking over an established musical rhetoric and then
progressively discovering that they could substitute a large num-
ber of different note-structures into the rhythmic-textural layout
of the old rhetoric and produce a musical effect that was not
only still recognizable as music but that emphasized more and
more the kind of character or expressive effect they were inter-
ested in. Thus chords based on the interval of the fourth and
symmetrical, parallel chords based on major and minor thirds
were substituted for the traditional tonal triads and their pro-
gressions.

The only people who were "at sea" were those, like myself
at first, who wanted to understand this new music in terms of

C major and so to analyze it in terms of a tonal context, when in many cases it had none, rather than of its musical-expressive character. Few people then saw that one could analyze a work in other terms than those of the tonal "system" and discover the way an atonal work had been constructed technically *in order to* make its musical-expressive point.

In creating musical character the essential underlying process would seem to consist, at the most general level, in the generation and release of tension by various means, whether it be a question of tonal or non-tonal music. This process, to summarize Leonard Meyer's well-known exposition, depends on: the creation of expectations in the listener; the subsequent affect- or tension-producing frustration of those expectations; and the final tension-releasing fulfillment of those expectations in more or less direct ways. The operation of this process is dependent, according to Meyer, on the playoff of musical elements in ways that the listener interprets in varying degrees as either "normal" (more or less according to expectation) or "deviant" (more or less contrary to expectation). Meyer demonstrates at length the specific manner of operation of such musical-psychological processes in the "tonal" style-system, as well as the historical evolution of the practice of "tonal" composers in treating a given morphological element either more as a "norm" or more as a "deviant" within the frame of the style-system as a whole in any of its particular periods.

The theoretical question—and also many practical questions—of post-tonal musical language would thus seem to depend for clarification upon the identification and isolation of its possible stylistic "norms"; unlike those of tonal music, these have seemed refractory to definition, when any conscious effort has been made in the past to pinpoint them for analytical and presumably autodidactic purposes.

About Leonard Meyer's ideas, let me say that every single piece of music sets up its own frame of norms and deviants, and that the only question about this is the "linguistic" level on which the identity of the piece and of its norms and deviants is es-

tablished. In "tonal music" there is obviously in most cases a
great deal of overlap between the vocabularies and syntaxes of
pieces written by different composers living around the same
time. Nonetheless, at a higher level of the continuum, a linguistic
differentiation always occurs that allows one to tell one piece
from the next. And, similarly, the more widely separated in
historical time given pieces of "tonal music" are, the more ge-
neric is the linguistic level at which differentiations appear. (For
example, Edward Lowinsky's comparison of a Bach fugue with
one of Mozart reveals how, within mutually accepted contra-
puntal patterns, the two differ quite obviously in their framing
of norms and deviants.) * In post-tonal music it's simply that
each composer, every time he writes a piece, has the opportunity
of "making up his own language," so to speak, conditioned only
by the requirement that it be a *language*, i.e., that from the point
of view of the imagined listener the morphological elements have
a recognizable identity in each case and that their status as mu-
tually relative "norms" and "deviants" (as Meyer puts it) be
clearly established in the work. It's perfectly obvious that the
liveliness of the operation of musical composition has always
been just this—the composer's finding or inventing a linguistic
"frame" for his piece that will make all the details come to life
in a new way. Clearly *Tristan* must have involved a terrific
operation of the intellect in terms of deciding what are the
"norms" of the piece. In a certain sense *Tristan* is involved en-
tirely with the various resolutions of the augmented sixth chord,
all of which had been used occasionally before—but never with
such frequency that they formed one of the essential elements
of a work. Indeed, from one point of view, you could almost
consider *Tristan* a "technical treatise" on this subject. In the
course of working on it, I can imagine Wagner writing out all
the possible surprising results you can get from resolving the
dominant seventh and augmented sixth chords in their many
enharmonic readings and then proceeding to find uses for them
in the actual opera. Thus this piece could be considered a kind
of game dealing with this particular musical problem, and hence
it is based on a particular set of norms and expectations that

* E. Lowinsky, "On Mozart's Rhythm," in *The Creative World of
Mozart,* ed. Paul Henry Lang, New York, 1963, pp. 31–33.

are not clear until you know the piece rather well, I would think. And this is certainly true of Beethoven just as much—the repeated D♯ in measure 10 of the Violin Concerto and the famous horn entrance in the "Eroica" Symphony are both extraordinarily surprising events that take a lot of hearing before one is convinced they are right, and not just something wayward and unconvincing.

And of course this leads to the question: how much can one violate the norms one has set up for a piece and still be convincing? It's obvious, for instance, that two measures of Dufay followed by two measures of Brahms would most likely violate one's first-established sense of continuity to such a point that the whole thing would cease to be convincing. This is a very important point in contemporary music, as in all music. It is one that was very seriously thought about, for instance, in the middle works of Haydn, where he was interested in making surprising continuities, which the listener would nonetheless always be able to comprehend as being part of a coherent overall musical development. Similarly in Couperin, one finds pieces like the *Croque-en-jambe*, in which every system of normative continuity is broken as the piece progresses and which yet remains convincing because Couperin builds up the discontinuities progressively, keeping in mind the one large linguistic frame and keeping the musical motion within it. The same kind of broken continuity occurs in the first movement of Bach's *Italian Concerto*.

Thus it seems to me that for a work to be convincing there has to be a large frame established in which, as I said, the "rules of the game" are presented. The deviations from the expected norms then must fall within this frame. Thus when I myself come to choosing a frame for a piece of music, while I like to include a very large repertory of different sorts of material, I always try to make them all conform at some level to one general sound character, so as to give the impression that they all belong together in the same piece. And similarly, while I believe that music should be continuously surprising, I believe it should be so in the sense that whatever happens should continue an already-perceived ongoing process or pattern, in a way that is convincing and yet also a way that the listener himself could nonetheless not have predicted before it actually happened. Thus my business as a composer, once I set something going, is to be sufficiently aware of the probable predictive expectations of the listener who has grasped the process I have begun, so as to be able to fulfill his expectations always in a way that is *both* surprising *and* convincing.*

Now none of this is a "logical" process in music in any mechanistic or purely abstract speculative sense but is based on essentially simple analogical principles whereby the listener perceives that this event is like this event, whereas that event is unlike this event but nevertheless part of the same work, and so on. On the basis of such comparisons, he develops expectations. The

---

* What I mean by this surprising but logical progression is repeatedly exemplified in the dialogues of Plato. In the *Sophist,* for instance, the Eleatic Stranger and the young Theaetetus decide to define what *sophist* means. The Stranger demonstrates rather at length the process of definition, using the term "angler" as an example. An angler is an artist, an acquisitive artist, a hunter, a hunter in the water, a fisher, a fisher that uses a hook. Then the Stranger says he will follow this same pattern in defining "sophist," but suddenly and surprisingly says that the angler and the sophist are cousins, they both are hunters; while the angler hunts in the water, the sophist hunts in rivers of wealth and broad meadow-lands of generous youth. This surprising shift of method is at first startling, like many moments in Haydn, but, as with the composer, Plato finally develops thoughts that make the sudden shift a convincing part of the argument, and with even greater skill leaves the reader at the end of the dialogue wondering whether he has been following the ingenious remarks of a sophist (the Stranger) or a true definition of a sophist. This amazing handling of sequences of thought in Plato—even to the Gertrude Stein–like *Parmenides*—never has stopped delighting me.

Of sophistry, of course, we have excellent examples everyday in the publicity that pollutes our minds, in education that ought to teach us to see the truth behind the preposterous claims of the "hunters" or "acquisitive artists" of our society but unfortunately often seems only to substitute one kind of sophistry for another. Sometimes, I must say, I myself feel as if I were a sophist when I yield to the pressure of educational institutions to talk about my work. It's a great temptation to invent "likely stories," as Socrates would say, to explain your own music when you have only been dimly aware, verbally, of what you were thinking while you were assembling expressive patterns of notes.

But the kind of urbane, amusing, penetrating dialogues Plato invented for Socrates so long ago take a very good writer (or speaker) and a great philosopher. I am afraid I am neither. So we will have to forge on in our slow way, hoping that some bits of useful information may help a few readers to understand something about what it is for one person, at least, to write music in the United States.

difficulty in much contemporary music is, of course, that most listeners are so unfamiliar with its vocabulary as to be unable to perceive events clearly and make the comparisons—even the initially quasi-subconscious ones—necessary to the development of a sense of musical continuity and, correlatively, of musical expectations on which the work depends for its effect.

Thus, as a serious composer, one has to write for a kind of intelligent and knowledgeable listener one seldom comes across in any number. But that the composer should nonetheless always try to think of the music he is writing, and of the means by which he is trying to achieve his communication, from the point of view of such an ideal listener remains no less paramount a requirement, in my opinion, simply because it seems to me that the real "composer" of any music is the listener who interprets it and makes sense of it—if any sense is to be made of it. And while the listener ideally should be as "good" as the composer, the composer himself, *if* he is to achieve his desired communication, must in every case be his own first ideal *listener*.

In connection with what you said about the importance of achieving a convincing and coherent continuity, how, from an analytical standpoint, do you feel this is specifically accomplished in a work like Schoenberg's Erwartung, *where the rapidity of change of texture from moment to moment would seem to pose this problem in a particularly radical way?*

Well, on the spur of the moment, I'm not able to analyze this in any detail, except to say that in addition to the presence of a literary text, which lends direction and connection to the musical events, the music itself is all based on and related almost continuously to—among other things—the three three-note chords that Schoenberg often used in writing his music of that period. Hence there is a sense of a unified sound-vocabulary provided by the pitch structure, no matter what the character of the rhythmic structure or of the textural layout (which, as you say, changes rapidly) at any given moment. A much more important factor that contributes to the "connectedness" of the continuity, no longer in this (so to speak) static way, but in a dynamic way

—the process that gives the work a sense of ongoing musical *motion*—is the over-all dynamic evolution of the whole piece, which, at the highest architectonic level, results in a "rhythm" of five or six large-scale tension-building crescendi with periods of relaxation in between.

In pointing here, as you do, to the role of "the sense of musical motion" in constituting the coherence of a musical continuity, you raise questions about the relation of music to time . . .

Any technical or esthetic consideration of music really must *start* with the matter of time. The basic problem has always been that analysts of music tend to treat its elements as static rather than as what they are—that is, *transitive* steps from one formation in time to another. All the materials of music have to be considered in relation to their projection in time, and by time, of course, I mean not visually measured "clock-time," but the medium through which (or way in which) we perceive, understand, and experience events. Music deals with this experiential kind of time, and its vocabulary must be organized by a musical syntax that takes direct account of, and thus can play on, the listener's "time-sense" (which in my opinion is a more illuminating way of referring to the "psychology of musical hearing").

This began to seem important to me around 1944, when I suddenly realized that, at least in my own education, people had always been consciously concerned only with this or that peculiar local rhythmic combination or sound-texture or novel harmony and had forgotten that the really interesting thing about music is the time of it—the way it all goes along. Moreover, it struck me that, despite the newness and variety of the post-tonal musical vocabulary, most modern pieces generally "went along" in an all-too-uniform way on their higher architectonic levels. That is, it seemed to me that, while we had heard every imaginable kind of harmonic and timbral combination, and while there had been a degree of rhythmic innovation on the *local* level in the music of Stravinsky, Bartók, Varèse, and

Ives particularly, nonetheless the way all this went together at the next higher and succeeding higher rhythmic levels remained in the orbit of what had begun to seem to me the rather limited rhythmic routine of previous Western music. This fact began to bother me enough so that I tried to think in larger-scale time-continuities of a kind that would be still convincing and yet at the same time *new* in a way commensurate with, and appropriate to, the richness of the modern musical vocabulary. This aim led me to question all the familiar methods of musical presentation and continuation—the whole so-called musical logic based on the statement of themes and their development. In considering constant change-process-evolution as music's prime factor, I found myself in direct opposition to the static repetitiveness of much early twentieth-century music, the squared-off articulation of the neoclassics, and indeed much of what is written today in which "first you do this for a while, then you do that." I wanted to mix up the "this" and the "that" and make them interact in other ways than by linear succession. Too, I questioned the inner shape of the "this" and the "that"—of local musical ideas—as well as their degree of linking and non-linking. Musical discourse, it became obvious to me, required as thorough a rethinking as harmony had been subjected to at the beginning of the century.

Now concretely, in the course of thinking about all of this, I once again—after many years' hiatus—took up interest in Indian *talas,* the Arabic *durub,* the "tempi" of Balinese *gamelans* (especially the accelerating *gangsar* and *rangkep*), and studied newer recordings of African music, that of the Watusi people in particular. At the same time the music of the early *quattrocento,* of Scriabin, and Ives, and the "hypothetical" techniques described in Cowell's *New Musical Resources* also furnished me with many ideas. The result in my own music was, first of all, the way of evolving rhythms and continuities now called "metric modulation," which I worked out during the composition of my Cello Sonata of 1948.* Now while, as I say, my thinking about

* There is nothing new about metric modulation but the name. To limit brief mention of its derivations to notated Western music: it is implicit in the rhythmic procedures of late fourteenth-century French music, as it is in music of the fifteenth and sixteenth centuries that uses hemiola

musical time was stimulated by a consideration of, among other
things, different kinds of rhythmic devices found in non-Western
music such as I have mentioned, I feel it is important to point
out that these devices interested me as suggestions of many syn-
tactical possibilities that would participate in a very rich and
varied large-scale rhythmic continuity such as is *never* found in
non-Western music, but *is* suggested by some aspects of Western
classical music, starting with Haydn especially. This aim of mine
is something very different from that of many European com-
posers who have been influenced by non-Western music and
who have tended to be interested in exotic rhythmic devices as
"things in themselves"—as local ideas more or less immediately
transposable into a (usually) extremely conventional and uninter-
esting over-all rhythmic framework derived from the simplest
aspects of older Western music and only slightly more varied
than that of the exotic music from which the local ideas have
been borrowed. As far as I am concerned, on the contrary,
what contemporary music needs is not just raw materials of
every kind but a way of relating these—of having them evolve
during the course of a work in a sharply meaningful way; that
is, what is needed is never just a string of "interesting passages,"
but works whose central interest is constituted by the way every-
thing that happens in them happens *as* and *when* it does in rela-
tion to everything else.

I feel very strongly about this, just because ever since 1944
I have realized that ultimately the matter of musical time is vastly
more important than the particulars or the novelty of the mu-
sical vocabulary, and that the morphological elements of any
music owe their musical effect almost entirely to their specific

---

and other ways of alternating meters, especially duple and triple. From then
on, since early sets of variations like those of Byrd and Bull started a
tradition of establishing tempo relationships between movements, metric
modulation began to relate movements of one piece together, as can be
seen in many works of Beethoven, not only in the variations of Op. 111, but
in many places where *doppio movimento* and other terms are used to in-
dicate tempo relationships. In fact, at that very time, the metronome was
invented, which establishes relationships between all tempi. In our time,
Stravinsky, following Satie, perhaps, wrote a few works around 1920 whose
movements were closely linked by a very narrow range of tempo relation-
ships, and much later Webern did the same.

"placing" in the musical time-continuity, just as perfectly ordinary and familiar details in a work of literature, like, say, the Library in Borges's *Library of Babel*, or the cockroach in Kafka's *Metamorphosis*, or the events (each commonplace enough) in K's life in *The Castle*, only take on the peculiar and gripping significance they have as a result of the manner and order in which they are juxtaposed and combined in the literary time-continuity. Indeed, scholars' "reshuffling" of the chapters of Kafka's *The Trial* and *The Castle* (in connection with a dispute over Max Brod's editing of these works) has not only rather radically altered their meaning and effect but by the same token has vividly demonstrated just how important time-continuity is, *precisely* in works that seem to depend on "discontinuity" for their character. And as I see it, much of the confusion that has arisen in recent discussion of this matter of musical time and, still more, in connection with the many and various mistaken compositional attempts to deal effectively with time in an actual work, has resulted from a refusal on the part of many composers to distinguish between, on the one hand, the given and inescapable structures of experiential time in accordance with which alone, the listener hears and grasps a piece of music (if he hears and grasps it at all); and, on the other hand, certain widespread secondary theorizings about time, of a kind that deny the irreversibility and even the very existence of time. It is certainly a question whether music, as the time-structure it is, can be made to present concretely such theorizings about time and still remain music, any more than a verbal language, say by the introduction of "blanks" or resorting to retrograde word-order, can convey a concrete idea of "non-temporal existence" or an experience (!) of "time going backwards." All verbal expressions and accounts of anything whatever, including time, require one letter and then one word after another for their presentation, and depend for their meaning on the specific ordering of the words, no matter how unconventional this ordering may be, just as music requires one sound after another in a determinate order for its presentation and for its particular effect on the listener, if any.

It seems to me that many of the works of the Darmstadt

school of composers have suffered greatly from the attempt
to apply certain mistaken "philosophic conceptions" of time to
music itself, though it is clear that the attractiveness of these con-
ceptions about, say, the "interchangeability of musical moments"
has its roots in the kind of visually- and spatially-derived mechan-
istic thinking that originally produced total serialism and was
unconcerned from the outset with the problem of time-conti-
nuity and of producing feelings of tension and release and there-
fore of musical motion in the listener, but dealt rather with
unusualness of aural effect, thus reducing music to mere physical
sound.

*You mention the word "moment," which has such prestige
of late . . .*

Just as I spoke about the elements of the musical vocabulary
being *transitive* steps in time, so on the next higher architectonic
level no "moment" can have any meaning except as a result
of its context, and can never be anything like the "epiphany"
the word seems to imply, when it is used in connection with
these other theories, unless it has been led up to so that it con-
stitutes a meaningful stage in a previously ongoing musical
process. In Joyce's *Dubliners,* in which the first conscious use
of this technique in a literary work was made, it's very obvious
that "epiphanies" occur always as a result of a situation in which
the person who is experiencing the events finally recognizes, in
a "moment of truth," what they all mean.

Of course this preoccupation with "moments" has a history
of its own in music. It is clear, for example, that a great deal of
late Romantic music was dedicated to the preparation for a
great moment of truth which, as the historical period approached
its end, more frequently failed to arrive—that is, a great deal
of tension was generated by very elaborate and long-winded
means and was then found to be incapable of convincing release
in terms of the accepted style. Partly for this reason, and partly
in reaction to the feeling that the "present" in music was being
entirely sacrificed to a "future" that was, among other things,
increasingly technically uncertain, Debussy and Schoenberg

became interested for a while in the possibilities of a musical
language which would live mainly "in the moment," so to speak,
and be based on tension-release periods of relatively short dura-
tion. The style they developed, of course, posed a problem the
minute they began to think of writing longer pieces, and I
must say that I find certain works like *Die glückliche Hand*
rather unconvincing on the formal level, just because they seem
like a collection of "moments" without the sense of propelling
interconnection one feels in *Erwartung,* for the reason I men-
tioned.

   Many of the recent "moment"-type works suffer from this,
in addition to the defect that many of the "moments," unlike
those in Schoenberg and Webern, are not even interesting in
themselves.

   *"Oriental music and philosophy" are often invoked in con-
nection with this trend . . .*

   One of the things I have felt about Oriental music, after
quite a good deal of experience with it, is that it is so terribly
lacking in variety and freedom. I have the impression that the
music of the most conservative Western composer—say, Gounod
—is much more free than any Oriental music I've ever heard,
because in Western music there are always multiple alternatives
for the composer to choose from on many levels, whereas there
are almost none but the very smallest ones in any given improv-
isation by such great performers as Ravi Shankar or the Dagar
brothers. No doubt that is one of the elements of its popularity
—like much Western popular music, Indian music is largely pre-
dictable on all but the lowest levels of its organization, at which
it may depend on the whim of the performer. In general this
seems to be true of most ethnic music too, especially that con-
nected with religion or magic. Gods and spirits are very con-
servative in their tastes, demanding *only* the correct ritual and
no other. Since they live so much longer than men, they can
keep their subjects from changing for thousands of years, as in
Pharaonic Egypt.

*It seems a particularly "Western" idea that time is not a
mere collection of isolated "moments," but rather a "story" with
a beginning and an end. Similarly, it seems a peculiarly Western
esthetic demand, related to the awareness of time as a "conse-
quential" process, that the rhythmic, tension-release pattern or
teleological structure of music should uninterruptedly motivate
and govern all the phenomena which, as a whole, are referred to
as a musical piece—in other words, that a piece should be a sin-
gle teleology seeking a single rhythmic completion rather than a
haphazard,* ad libitum *series of micro-teleologies exhausting
themselves rhythmically in a matter of seconds.*

Well, just as it's obvious that this sort of teleological think-
ing has historically been very strong in Western civilization, it's
obvious that today there are many people who are not particu-
larly happy with it and who wish either simply not to be part
of it or to find other ways of thinking. I feel that in my own
music I have been dealing with a kind of time-awareness that is
not part of the *familiar* teleological method, especially the usual
story-telling kind.* Now, it's very hard to do this; I'm not sure

---

* There are, of course, two levels of musical teleology which could be
considered. The first is a "linguistic" one—one sound follows another and
another, and this "adds up" to an entity in time, just as phonemes can
add up to words, then sentences. This is, in my mind, as I have said, the
condition of any temporal kind of communication. It is in a sense teleological,
in the same way that life or pure existence is, one moment being the cause
of the next. Now, it is possible to string along a series of vocal sounds that
do not produce any language the speaker or listener knows. This is still con-
strued as communication—affecting tones, assonances, pauses, and so on are
sought for by the listener in an attempt to piece this together into a teleologi-
cal scheme, albeit a frustrating and low-level one. (The discussion of aphasia
by Roman Jakobson is particularly interesting on this.) Secondly, there is the
large-scale teleology of story-telling, of coming to the point, to a climax every
so often. And a third might be considered—that of intentionality, the final
cause of the work.
  The whole cause-and-effect pattern, as I pointed out in the program
notes for my *Variations,* is only one process of change—or one interpretation
of change. While I am a little fed up (and have been for quite a while) with
Gide's and Camus's *acte gratuit,* still it is another such pattern (albeit inter-
esting primarily as an intellectual concept and an ethical problem involving
the relationships of people). In any case we are always finding that the effect
resulting from a cause is quite different from what we expected. Also, I follow
Alfred North Whitehead in believing that existence of any kind is a teleo-

I have succeeded completely, but that has been one of my aims. After all, we were very aware in the twenties and thirties of contemporary music that was very repetitious and attempted to produce an effect of static hypnosis, somewhat similar to that of some Oriental music. This was something to which, as an adolescent, I was particularly sympathetic, but soon felt the desire to break from. What I most wanted to do, subsequently, was to find new kinds of musical motion.

So much vehemence is attached to the arguments advanced by certain "aleatoric" composers in purported justification of the "free-floating moment" and other "time theories" that one suspects something afoot in these appeals to, for example, "historical necessity," other than clear-sighted appraisal of the compositional situation . . .

Of course, I'm old-fashioned enough to believe that a great deal of this talk comes from people who are not willing to be responsible and face the consequences of a finite action. To me this is a frustrating way to exist. I understand why people do it —life is very confusing, and it's very hard to decide anything; our society constantly destroys the clarity of all issues, and as a result it's very hard to take a stand. The next step is simply to say, "Well, to hell with it all. Whether it's this way or that, it's all the same." (After a bad performance, I feel the same way.)

On another level, one wonders if the education of these composers was faulty, insofar as it allowed them to overlook the basic fact of over-all time-continuity in the works they studied as models when students.

What we're discussing now can easily lead to what might seem like a very "reactionary" point of view. The classics of

---

logical process, in which various kinds of concrescences attain and then later lose integrated patterns of feeling. "The ultimate creative purpose" is "that each unification shall achieve some maximum depth of intensity of feeling, subject to the conditions of its concrescence." These conditions vary, of course, depending on whether the existence in question is a physical object, a state of mind, a work of art, or a transcendent being.

music are a good demonstration of musical motion in a broad and interesting way, but one which at a certain point came to seem dead and conventional. There was a violent reaction against this feeling of deadness, which unfortunately took the form, in some respects, of a disinterest in, or incapacity to think of, ways of producing a sense of musical motion by means that were *not* dead, and which had indeed never been tried. Hence, partly also under the influence of medieval and non-Western music, composers often fell back into static conceptions and methods of working, which must have seemed to many to offer the simplest "solution" to the problems of post-tonal musical composition. That we're *still* living under the stars of this by-now reactionary aspect of the atonal revolution is depressingly obvious and explains the fact that although the Viennese composers like Schoenberg and Berg occasionally did devise a new kind of dynamic continuity, still, in the end, they have always been put down by some as "old-fashioned," probably precisely because they were not static.

You mention Schoenberg and Berg—were there other composers whose works were suggestive to you in thinking specifically about the problem of musical time?

Well, as I mentioned earlier, Haydn, also Beethoven to a certain extent, and Mozart to a much greater degree—all of them were concerned with this problem precisely in their preoccupation with degrees of contrast, of alternation and successive growth, of disjunction and so on.

Then too, among more recent composers, Debussy has been an important and thought-provoking influence, *not* in respect of the static-repetitious side of his music, which is "analyzed" so much, but because of the remarkable overall time-sweep of his pieces, mainly the later ones like *Jeux* and the three sonatas. I recall giving a lecture on these works at Princeton, in 1947, which perplexed everyone because I said that there Debussy was experimenting with a new kind of form. I think this is true, and to me it is certainly the most original and interesting aspect of his music, considered technically.

Stravinsky's works, particularly those coming after 1930, have also interested me from just this point of view, which is one of the many musical reasons why I awaited the appearance of each of his new works with the most intense curiosity and expectation ever since 1925, when I heard *The Rite of Spring* for the first time.

My interest and thinking about musical time were also very much stimulated by the kinds of "cutting" and continuity you find in the movies of Eisenstein, particularly *Ten Days That Shook The World* and *Potemkin,* and such as are described in his books, *Film Sense* and *Film Form.* I was similarly interested by the onward-moving continuity in the ballets of George Balanchine—every individual momentary tableau in the best of his ballets is something that the viewer has seen interestingly evolved, yet is also only a stage of a process that is going on to another point; and, while every moment is a fascinating and beautiful thing in itself, still what's much more fascinating is the continuity, the way each moment is being led up to and led away from—something you are not aware of in the ballets of most other choreographers as being anything of interest or which has even been thought about much. Indeed, the Balanchine ballets have been very stimulating to me in this way ever since 1933, when I saw many of them in Paris. They have been important as an example, in another art, of what one might do with music: one wanted to have very vivid moments, but what was more interesting was the process by which these moments came into being and by which they disappeared and turned into other moments.

It has been remarked that you are today one of the only advanced composers who really thinks of music in a contrapuntal way. Is this way of thinking specifically related to your feelings about time-continuity and musical form?

Well, this question has a number of angles. To begin with, while it's obvious that the constant and over-all phenomenon of music is one in which every "moment" is in the process of coming from some previous moment and leading to some future moment—only *thus* contributing to what is happening in the present—it seems to me that this process can have a number of simultaneous dimensions such that, for example, the moment, as it occurs, may consist of a number of simultaneously-evolving event patterns or sub-continuities of more or less radically different musical character, which interreact with each other to produce a "total" continuity and character-effect (which, as the dialectical synthesis of the contributing sub-continuities and characters, is irreducible to any one of these or to any "sum" of their qualities). It seems to me that this is very much the way we think all the time and that the feeling of experience is always the synthesis of our awareness of half-a-dozen simultaneous different feelings and perceptions all interreacting together, with now one and now another coming into the main focus while the others continue, more or less in the background, to influence it and give it the intellectual and affective meaning it has.

Though it's true that I did an enormous amount of strict counterpoint with Nadia Boulanger, I don't feel that this really accounts for the kind of thing I now do in my own music —because at a certain point I decided that the traditional categories, like "theme and accompaniment," or "subject and counter-subject," really didn't deal with what began to seem to me the vast spectrum of kinds of relationship that the contributory vertical elements in the musical continuity can have with each other in respect of the past and future of the piece. That is, it's obvious that a great deal of the texture in older music (and in most contemporary music) results from a desire for "fat" as related to "thin" sounds (or, to be more up-to-date, various degrees of textural density) within a *single*, vertically homogenous stream of continuity—while it seems to me that this is only one possibility, and not a terribly interesting one. What began to interest me was the possibility of a texture in which, say, massive vertical sounds would be entirely composed of simultaneous elements having a direct and individual horizontal relation to the whole progress or history of the piece—that is, simultaneous elements, each of which has its own way of leading from the previous moment to the following one, maintaining its identity as part of one of a number of distinct, simultaneously evolving, contributory thought-processes or musical characters. Hence I began as early as 1944, in works like my *Holiday Overture*, to think in terms of simultaneous streams of different things going on together, rather than in terms of the usual categories of counterpoint and harmony.

In trying to deal with this idea in a viable way I've used many different methods—such as producing a texture of musical layers or streams in which the progression of one is slow and another fast, or in which one is very spasmodic and another very continuous, and so on; sometimes, in fact, the total notion of the piece is derived directly from this idea of simultaneously interacting heterogeneous character-continuities, as in my Second String Quartet. In these cases, the principal idea is a sort of generalized program concerned with one aspect of the formal structure, whereby the trajectory of the whole piece, its progression or rise and fall of tension in time, from its beginning to its end, is produced by the interaction of the contributory elements. The coordination of these contrasting layers of music then forms an integral part of the musical discourse of the work and gives it its small and large formal evolution. (The form I seek is Coleridge's "form as proceeding," and I try to avoid "shape as superinduced." For the latter, as he says, "is either the death or the imprisonment of the thing; the former is its self-witnessing and self-effected sphere of agency.")

There are a number of striking historical examples of this kind of thing in opera, particularly in Mozart and late Verdi, where, for example, the musical structure and character of many scenes result from the simultaneous interaction of a number of very different musical sub-continuities. You only have to think of the finale of the second act of *Falstaff*, where Sir John is thrown out the window by the merry wives: here, the love music of Nannetta and Fenton, the gasps of Sir John, the jealousy of Ford, and the gay-hearted prattle of the wives are all simultaneously interwoven to express a whole cosmos of ideas about love, age, and so on, and draw together musical material from other places in the work. Similarly, the finale of the first act of *Don Giovanni* achieves its extraordinary musical and dramatic character thanks to this particular kind of simultaneous

multi-layered continuity, involving three on-stage dance or-
chestras simultaneously playing dances for the three estates of
society, each of which is seen dancing while Don Giovanni sings
a pseudo-revolutionary hymn. In this, it's a good deal like a
movie in which you see a lot of people at once, and then close-
ups of each one of them, so that you're aware of what each per-
son is like and what they're doing, and then later you are shown
how they all contribute to a large pattern of interaction.

Often the formal notion of my pieces is exactly that kind of
thing—for example, in my Concerto for Orchestra there is a
vertical division into four main character-movements, which are
all going on simultaneously, each one successively fading in and
out of prominence relative to the others. This fading into and out
of highlight provides a kind of "close-up" of elements that con-
tribute to a total effect, and which are thus, as it were, picked out
of a welter of things and contemplated carefully while the welter
continues to press in on them, and gives them, "dialectically," a
special new meaning.*

* Counterpoint, polyphony, and their study are very interestingly
commented on by Mahler in several remarks quoted by Natalie Bauer-Lechner
in her *Erinnerungen an Gustav Mahler,* and discussed by Theodor W. Adorno
in his book on the composer. Mahler regretted that he had been
excused from the counterpoint classes at the Vienna Conservatory because
of his outstanding youthful compositions, because as time passed, especially
from the Fourth Symphony onwards, he realized that he was becoming more
and more of a polyphonic composer and began to feel, as he recalled Schu-
bert did at the end of his life, that he should study this discipline more
rigorously. His attitude toward polyphony, toward simultaneity of different
materials, is curiously like that of Ives. Frau Bauer-Lechner describes a
Festtag when she and Mahler climbed a mountain together: when they were
at a certain height, he stopped, hearing the festive sounds, bands, and a
men's chorus coming from different directions, and exclaimed, "Das ist die
eigentliche Polyphonie!" ("That is the true polyphony"), enjoying both the
disconnectedness of the different musical materials and also the fact that
they were metrically uncoordinated. It reminded him of treasured child-
hood experiences, just as similar situations did Ives. "Do you hear it?
It's 'true polyphony,' and it's here that I get my own polyphonic sense.
In my earliest childhood in the forest of Iglau I was deeply moved and
impressed by just such a complex of sounds. For it is the very same thing
whether it sounds forth in such a tumult as this, in the thousand-fold in-
terwoven singing of birds, in the howling of storms, in the lapping of waves
or in the crackling of flames. In just this way must musical themes make
their appearance from completely different directions and be just so sharply
distinguished in rhythmic and melodic outline (anything less is mere textual

Now the order in which such simultaneous layers are first introduced or subsequently presented in highlight is extremely important, because if you present Layer A in highlight first, it will have a different effect when it becomes secondary to Layer B than if it only first emerges from a prior highlighted appearance of Layer B. Thus, as I said earlier, I take exactly the opposite stand from those composers of every stripe who don't believe the order of presentation is important in music and who don't appear to recognize that this order influences and in fact confers the meaning and effect that a given set of musical events comes to possess—or who, recognizing this, don't appear to know or care what their music is to mean and what effect it is to have (unless, as is rarely the case, they are very ingenious and compose in such a way that each version is meaningful).*

In connection with an earlier question about "rational criteria" in musical composition, your reference just now to opera seems particularly significant in that it tends to point toward a necessary connection between the nature of musical time and the idea of drama in the most general sense. That is, in music one doesn't just have, say, a chord because it's a sonority or because one has had it already a million times in the piece, but because it has some dramatic significance and effect coming where and as it does.

Yes, one tries to make every event, every kind of material, have its own particular kind of significance in the musical continuity. And furthermore, since we no longer have a given set of chords and rhythmic patterns possessing a partially "foreor-

---

padding and disguised homophony): the only difference is that the composer takes these several strands and organizes them into a coordinated and unified whole." Natalie Bauer-Lechner, *Erinnerungen an Gustav Mahler,* Leipzig-Vienna-Zurich, 1923, p. 147.

* Of course, the order of presentation of sections of music of any size is often not very critical, as for instance in the central movements of Baroque suites, classical serenades and cassations, and even some symphonies. While with Beethoven, Schubert, Schumann, and Brahms the sections or movements seem in many cases less interchangeable, with Stravinsky, as in *The Rite of Spring,* only the order given by the composer would make sense. This might be less true of certain neoclassical works of Schoenberg and Hindemith.

dained" set of constructive and expressive meanings of this sort, we have to invent everything point by point toward this end. This is why the present era of music is much more interesting in its possibilities than any period in the past—we suddenly have this enormous vocabulary, which musicians haven't begun, in most cases, to deal with on any but the lowest, momentary levels of musical significance.

When you begin to think about composing a new work, do you find yourself imagining specific, so to speak, "local" ideas or passages, or do you start with something more over-all and general?

In answering such a question I find one of the problems is that I write each of my works in a different way. I usually have at first a very specific plan of evolution for the whole of the work, with many of the details of the local events only very generally in mind. That is, I usually start with an idea of the sound, the musical character, and the dramatic development of these, similar to the plot—or subject—outline of a novel or play, or the scenario of a movie.

Yet in the case of the Double Concerto I began to conceive the work in terms of the "given," which was at first a request to write a piece for harpsichord and piano. In thinking of how these rather dissimilar sound-characters could be related to each other, I shortly arrived at the idea of unpitched percussion groups, from which everything the two soloists did could be rhythmically derived. According to this notion, a "primordial rhythm" expressed by the unpitched percussion would progressively take on pitches through the two resonating solo instruments, whose statements would then be elaborated and amplified by two groups of sustaining pitched instruments. Finally, at the beginning of a "coda," there was to be a gong crash, whose vibrating complex of resonances would be "orchestrated," as it died away, by the pitched instruments, which would then be progressively reabsorbed by the unpitched percussion. Thus, the first stage of conception was the general dramatic plan of a constellation of musical materials and ideas coming into existence, achieving focus and greater differentiation, then finally dissolving again and disintegrating into nothing. The next stage was that of working out this over-all plan concretely; and determining the specific rhythmic detail-patterns of the basic material, and how they could be variously combined and interrelated, and how they could acquire pitch. All the time during these technical considerations, an expressive and meaning structure was developing that gave point to the instrumental combination.

Now, while the Piano Concerto is entirely different in conception, there was again from the beginning an over-all notion of the work—the dramatic idea of a conflict between the pianist, whose part emphasizes sensitivity, variety of feeling, and virtuosity, and the orchestra, which progressively dissociates itself from the piano part, becoming increasingly insensitive, unvaried, and brutal—in terms of which all the specific local events and details were subsequently determined. Hence, no specific event or passage was thought of primarily "for its own sake," but always as a means toward the realization and communication of the fundamental dramatic idea of the work.

Thus the formal "outcome" of your works is never in doubt when you come to the actual composition . . .

Not on the highest architectonic level. On the next highest level, however, I'm often very unsure what I will do specifically until I get to the passage in question in the course of composition. For example, in the Piano Concerto I was already very far into the piece before I began to have a very clear idea what detailed form the end of the second movement would have, though I had known from the outset that I wanted a kind of "cyclone" effect preceding a short final piano solo. What I usually do, when I come to the actual writing of a given passage, is to propose to myself, at varying levels of specificity, many different realizations of the general idea to which the passage is to conform. Thus sometimes I actually sketch out many possible concrete solutions to the same general conception, until I finally get the one that satisfies me. I find to my chagrin that this is never done rapidly, which is why it takes me so long to write my works.

*How do you feel about the idea of dealing musically with a
literary text which already presents a dramatic structure of its
own?*

It is difficult to find a text that I would like to set to
music. Let me say that I have the offer of a rather large and ex-
pansive commission for which I could finally do the thing I've
thought about for a good part of my life, which is to make an
oratorio out of Hart Crane's magnificent poem *The Bridge*. But
now I'm not sure I want to do it, partly because I find that the
speed of presentation in words is very different from the speed
of presentation in my music. Also, I don't understand words
very well when they're sung, which is a troublesome prob-
lem. It seems to me that vocal music in general has to be rethought
completely and that I don't have the time or the patience to do
that single-handedly. Then too, it takes me so long to write my
pieces that I would hate to write one that I might end up feeling
was a wasted effort. And while there are many experiments I
would like to try if they could be set up in a couple of days and
then abandoned if they didn't work out, part of the business of
imagining any piece of music at all, as I see it, is imagining the
whole mode of expression and thought and working out a time-
structure—all of which just can't be done overnight. And then
with a text there is a whole other time-structure to be thought
of and dealt with, something I'm not sure I could teach myself
to work with now without wasting a large amount of effort. The
same is true of electronic music, which I think has many possi-
bilities.

*Turning for a moment to somewhat more circumscribed
technical questions, how have you dealt with the matter of pitch
structure in your works, and what functional role has this played
in relation to the other dimensions of the musical rhetoric with
which you are involved?*

Well, in all my works from the Cello Sonata up through
the Double Concerto I used specific chords mainly as unify-

ing factors in the musical rhetoric—that is, as frequently re-
curring central sounds from which the different pitch material of
the pieces was derived. For example, my First String Quartet is
based on an "all-interval" four-note chord, which is used con-
stantly, both vertically and occasionally as a motive to join all
the intervals of the work into a characteristic sound whose
presence is felt "through" all the very different kinds of linear
intervallic writing. This chord functions as a harmonic "frame"
for the work in just the sense I meant earlier, in talking about the
necessity of establishing a linguistic frame which makes all the
events and details of a piece of music feel as if they belong to-
gether and constitute a convincing and unified musical continuity.

In the case of the Double Concerto, there are two such four-
note all-interval chords, one for each of the two instrumental
character groups. (There are, incidentally, only these two all-
interval chords possible in our chromatic system.) Here the
all-interval chords serve not only a unifying function, in the
above-mentioned sense, but also a demarcating or identifying
function. The unifying aspect results from the fact that whatever
goes on in detail in either of these character-groups is derived
from and referrable to their respective "governing" all-interval
chords. The demarcating function results from the difference
between the characteristic sounds of these two chords, and of the
mutually inverse intervals composing each of them (for example,
harpsichord group: minor second; piano group: major seventh;
and so on), which thus serve to keep the two musical character-
groups "harmonically" distinct as entities.

Now, while this method of harmonic framing and demarca-
tion persists in my more recent works, it takes on a considerably
expanded form. This has to do with the fact that in all my pieces
written before the Piano Concerto the pitch-behavior of the sub-
voices constituting the separate contributing characters was almost
entirely linear or built up of two-note intervals, whereas the
Piano Concerto is very often densely chordal. Thus in the Double
Concerto, though the two character-groups are demarcated and
individually unified by characteristic chord-sounds, the different
sub-voices within each of these character groups (almost always
defined by a certain metronomic speed) are "harmonically" dif-

ferentiated only by characteristic single intervals, whereas in the Piano Concerto these sub-voices themselves are also differentiated by characteristic chord-sounds. That is, in the Piano Concerto not only are the piano and orchestra as character-identities distinguished by respective identifying twelve-note chords, but the different speed-layers of each character are distinguished by identifying three-note chord-sounds, derived in each case from the relevant character-identifying twelve-note chord. (Here also, there is a separation or complementarity of intervals between groups.) The same is true in my new Concerto for Orchestra, where I used sounds composed of five and seven notes instead of three.

This has become for me a whole new field of thought, involving such questions as what two-note groups are contained in three-note groups, and so forth. This way of working allows me to make all sorts of harmonic identities by adding and subtracting notes and so produce a whole gamut of harmonic colors all related to each other. This seems to me a far more serviceable and flexible way of dealing with pitch relations than the twelve-tone method, because while the latter provides the kind of linguistic frame that Schoenberg was looking for when he devised it, mine has none of the rigidity that has to be fought against by users of the method and is in fact in this respect much closer to the way of working with pitches that Schoenberg was already using in the atonal works he wrote before he became preoccupied with "series," and also closer to certain later works of the three Viennese in which three- or four-note segments of the row are treated as groups that could be given different orders.

How precisely do you expect the listener to be able to follow consciously the subtle graduations of color that are possible with thick twelve-note, or even five- and seven-note combinations, and how do you see this as differing from the problem of following set transformations in serial music?

Well, I seldom use the twelve-note vertical combination as a simultaneous chord in the Piano Concerto, and when I do, I always use it in the same vertical interval-order, so that it constitutes a fixed sound that is recognizable to the listener. When the work was played in Minneapolis, I gave a lecture with the orchestra on the stage and had examples played to show how each of the different chords contributed to the work. I was surprised at how easy it was to follow.

The question of how much you can expect most listeners to hear is a problem in itself—I wonder how many people hear themes coming back in the tonic in a Beethoven symphony. And furthermore, Beethoven himself, with functional harmony at his disposal, always presented many effects coordinated with the return of themes to the tonic at the beginning of a recapitulation— some emphatic non-harmonic effect such as, for instance, a pause or a long pedal, so that when the theme returns in the tonic it's very obvious that *something* has happened, whether a listener recognizes it's the tonic or not. Similarly, I use coordinations of different sorts to articulate the flow of musical ideas in my own works.

The question of coordinations is an interesting one, I mean the question of how many "parameters" have to be coordinated, and in what way, in order to produce a noticeable and meaningful effect. The serialists, in many cases, don't believe anything has to be coordinated except by the random combinations of number systems—which leads to the kind of permutations that are heard as a chaotic uniformity. Yet I believe there are an infinite number of possible new convincing coordinations, and in my music the harmonic sounds are closely related to tempos and rhythmic ideas to form characteristic kinds of events that are distinct and followable, not only because of their pitch-structure but because of their other coordinated aspects.

To what degree is "absolute pitch" a factor in the structure of your music? In particular, are the repeated F's in the second movement of your Piano Concerto specifically meant to be heard as being related to previously sounded F's at that registral level?

No, the F was chosen in no more complicated way than that F was more or less the middle note of the whole big string sound-effect at that point, which was crowding the piano out, reducing its part to almost nothing. Its important relation is not to other F's but to other repeated notes, like the E♭ heard previously which, being a whole step lower, "leads" after many measures to F.

The actual notion of "absolute pitch" is not significant in my pieces. The pitches are chosen registrally as a matter of instrumental practicality. In fact, I frequently transpose parts of my pieces up and down, when I compose them, to try and decide in just which register they would sound most characteristic, given the instruments that are playing them. I make a decision on this basis and in consideration of the degree of expressivity of the given passage as compared with the preceding and succeeding passages.

Given your disinterest in the kind of "occult" retrogrades and inversions of pitch ideas found in serial music, one is surprised to find near the beginning of the second movement of your Piano Concerto an inversion of a rapid piano figure that had appeared earlier, near the end of the first movement. Is this meant to be grasped consciously by the listener, and are there many other such happenings in the piece?

Actually there are few others. I thought of this inversion as a way of "destroying the technique" of the first movement, so to speak, of getting away from the first movement's character and atmosphere by slow degrees, preserving, in this case, the rhythmic figure intact but inverting the pitch succession and transposing the whole thing up so that none of the pitches would be identical with those of the previous appearance of the figure. In the first movement that twelve-note chord on which the figure is based always appeared in the same form, with the interval of the sixth always on the bottom, and so on. This time, I thought, now the sixth will be on top. In other words, I wanted the second movement to become a very free treatment of materials that in the first movement had been restricted to a more limited pattern of behavior, and to open out into a broader, more expressive character, encompassing the three woodwind solos—false comforters to the piano's Job.

To turn to the area of rhythm, you have spoken on various public occasions about sections of certain of your pieces, notably the Double Concerto and second movement of your Piano Concerto, in such a way as to suggest that these were conceived as "giant" polyrhythms, from whose individual terms detail-structures and local events hang suspended, as it were. If this is so, to what extent and in what way do you feel such very large-scale rhythmic processes can or should be consciously perceived, and how do you reconcile this process, whose working-out might appear "mechanical," with your concern for dramatic continuity?

Well, it seemed very obvious to me that in older music the "periodic effect" of multiples of two and three beats was used with great power, and could also be modified with enormous effect. For instance, Beethoven began to use larger rhythmic periods as actual architectonic elements—such as the repeated chords at the beginning of the "Eroica" Symphony and at the ends of movements. These chords at the ends of movements give the impression that the music has been emptied of everything but the "marking time" of these big periods of grandly epic scale.

Furthermore, I was aware that one of the big problems of contemporary music was that irregular and other kinds of rhythmic devices used in it tended to have a very small-scale cyclical organization—you heard patterns happening over one or two measures and no more. For this reason, one of the things I became interested in over the last ten years was an attempt to give the feeling of both smaller and larger-scale rhythmic periods. One way was to set out large-scale rhythmic patterns before writing the music, which would then become the important stress points of the piece, or section of a piece. These patterns or cycles were then subdivided in several degrees down to the smallest level of the rhythmic structure, relating the detail to the whole.*

* To go into somewhat more detail, I should point out that at this latter, most highly subdivided level—the level of the fastest succession of local rhythmic attacks—I never use (as other composers have often done) rapid polyrhythms of a ratio higher than I think playable and distinguishable for the listener at the speed in question. Thus, even though it is obvious that by mechanical means all sorts of rapid polyrhythms can be pro-

Thus I certainly don't expect the listener to be able to hear the exact *numerical* relations of the cyclical structure of, say, the coda of my Double Concerto, which has one orchestra moving in cycles of seven measures and the other in cycles of five measures, yet I'm sure he will clearly hear an interesting, irregular rhythmic interrelation between the two groups as they fade in and out relative to each other at different speeds, and that he will hear this taking place and keeping up tension over a long stretch of the continuity. This cyclical structure is thus one of the means by which I have hoped to give a certain kind of large dynamic continuity to my music even to the point where in the Concerto for Orchestra the four simultaneous movements fade in and out according to a very large-scale cyclical plan of this sort which on the highest level governs everything from beginning to end.

I should emphasize again that I don't particularly care about the listener being able to perceive that there are "polyrhythms"

---

duced, and even though it's quite easy to imagine all kinds of ways of coordinating local rhythmic patterns by serialization and other mechanical means, I have nevertheless abstained from such purely speculative and abstract elaborations and have limited myself on the local level to the simplest polyrhythmic combinations. This comes out of consideration for the fact that, just as the ear tends to assimilate microtonal intervals larger than the minor second to the nearest familiar interval, so too it not only tends to assimilate the initial and terminal stages of a higher-ratio polyrhythm to the cycle of a more easily recognized polyrhythm, such as 3:2, but also tends to hear a very rapidly moving higher-ratio polyrhythm as a mere blur of notes whose precise rhythmic relations have no specific tension-value. It is *only* at more moderate and slow tempi that a large-ratio polyrhythm begins to have clearly perceptible tension-value, such that a polyrhythm like 71:49 starts off sounding like a 3:2 but then clearly begins to get out of phase and then to get back into phase in a perceptually transparent way. Thus, what I have often done in my more recent pieces is to have the eventual rapid polyrhythmic cycles of, say, 6:7 on the smallest rhythmic level each be single beats or terms of a much higher-ratio polyrhythmic cycle, such as 71:49, occurring at a much slower speed on the next higher rhythmic level of the passage in question. In this way one has not only the local rhythmic tension provided by the fast cycles of 6:7, but also a rhythmic tension on a much larger scale resulting from the getting-out-of-the-phase and getting-back-into-phase of the slower-moving beats each constituted by one of these fast-moving cycles of 6:7.

Now, at no rhythmic level of the pieces or passages in question are these polyrhythms carried out always literally and mechanically, but rather they all simply form elements of a flexible musical syntax aimed solely and immediately at perception.

going on, and which particular ones there are. The effect I am interested in producing is, as I have said, one of perceived large-scale rhythmic tension, sometimes involving the anticipation of an impending final coincidence of all the disparate rhythmic layers at some key moment. This occurs on a rather elaborate scale in the second movement of the Piano Concerto, in which there are many layers of rhythm going on very slowly, none of them coinciding until finally they all seem to come together on that very loud chord at measure 615. Now, while this final coincidence has been led up to over a matter of fifty or sixty measures beforehand, it has not been brought about in any literal or mechanical way—I conceived of this general plan as an "idea," but when it came to working it out concretely, I found that, if the regularity of the gradual approach to the "zero-point" of rhythmic unison were too obvious, it would lose a good deal of its effect, and so I began to work at realizing the idea in a more imaginative way. That is, the important thing was that the large-scale process which approaches resolution should be continuously interesting in detail and make its ominously dramatic point.

How do you feel about the possible risk that such a process, tremendously distended over great stretches of time, might tend to give the textural impression of "pointillism" rather than polyphony?

The impression of "pointillism" results, as I see it, from the failure of orchestral musicians to observe the written dynamics that keep the slow-moving voices distinct as voices. This is extremely important if the intended effect is to be realized. Orchestral musicians, however, tend to be very skeptical of indications that tell them to play something at a different dynamic level than the one at which their neighbors are playing, since they are so used to producing the mass effects called for by much tonal music popular with the public. This is the penalty one pays for writing polyphonic music, I suppose.

Nevertheless, when the music is correctly executed, as I am aware from experience, the point is clearly made and the large-scale polyrhythmic process quite naturally has the effect I've

spoken of, especially since in the Piano Concerto the same process
is presented many times, usually in a fragmentary way, at the
most easily graspable speeds, long before it begins to be presented
on a "grand" scale. Thus, the listener should begin to grasp the
slow beats as parts of such a process soon after it starts.

Then too, one of the things I like about this kind of effect
at slow speeds is that at first these points of rhythm *don't* seem
to have any graspable relation to each other and appear per-
plexing or perhaps chaotic, pointillist if you like. Then, as these
beats begin to converge toward a unison, you begin to become
aware of their pattern and to grasp the emerging rhythmic con-
vergences. Conversely, the rhythm may at first appear clearly
directional and structured and then seem to disintegrate into a
floating, apparent incoherence. This sense of progression into
extreme irregularity and back to a perceptible order appears in
many of my works. One of the things I hope to achieve is that
it be audible from a number of different points of view, and
heard many times, with new and different things observed in it
on each occasion. There is meant to be a sense of layers of mean-
ing, resulting from a desire to achieve a richness of reference
in unfamiliar ways. Hence these polyrhythmic passages, which
at times give the effect of almost hysterical disorganization, are
in the end part of a graspable order, and if they can be heard in
both ways, it's what I want. It's kind of terrifying in a way—
you see, I always deal with things that have a very strong
dramatic meaning to myself, and the conflict of chaos and order
is particularly significant because it seems to be at the root of so
many of the things important to us.

*You have often spoken of the difficulty of establishing a
satisfactory pedagogy for composers who are now students.
Also, in talking about the technical grounds of your own mu-
sic, you disclaim any probable usefulness of the techniques you
yourself have invented, for any other composer . . .*

It's very difficult for me to deal with the education of a
young composer without stirring up the whole question of edu-
cation itself. As you can see from what I said about my own

education, I had, at the time when I was attending educational institutions, the impression that I was learning very little about what I cared about most: modern music, the issues of contemporary life and art. I made a great effort to learn about these on my own, in high school, college, and in Paris, sometimes to the detriment of my "official" studies. It is still very hard for me to imagine that students can be expected to learn a great deal from their courses. In the end, everyone who really cares about a subject ends up teaching himself what he wants to learn. Courses at Harvard had to be passed so that I could stay there and study the scores of Stravinsky and Bartók, read *transition* and *La Révolution surréaliste,* and talk to others who were similarly interested—and hear concerts, see plays and art exhibits, and take part in political discussions and actions, and all sorts of other things.

I am always surprised when students in the fields of music and art show so little initiative in learning for themselves. Courses usually skim along over subjects—especially contemporary ones, now that these are part of art-teaching—and give pat, often unconvincing answers (understandably) about the matters that arise in connection with them, because these do not yet benefit from the kind of intellectual distance and thought that characterizes our relation to older works.

It is for this reason that I tend to suspect many modern attempts to devise new pedagogic systems for contemporary music (or any other art, for that matter). They can be dangerous both to the student, who can be typecast in a certain style that he cannot escape from, and to the artist or composer who devises such a system. We've witnessed a composer like Hindemith sink under the effort of trying to base his pedagogy on his own music, and end up basing his music on his own pedagogy.

Furthermore, I have the feeling that if I myself ever found a way of teaching what I do in my music, I'm not sure I wouldn't stop writing that way. I feel strongly enough about this so that I've been very hesitant even to describe how I write my pieces, and it's only been recently, often many years after they were written, that I've begun to do this. I recall an occasion at Princeton in 1959 when I said something about the all-interval chord I used in my First String Quartet, and a young professor jumped up and said, "I'm the only one who's ever used that—I discovered it!" I said, "Well, I wrote this piece ten years ago," and he said, "No, really?"

Another problem of pedagogical methods based on recent techniques is that these techniques seem so much involved with the specific pieces in which they turn up. Then too, most people don't have the same point of view that I do about how to write music, so that I'm not sure that my way of working would be worth rationalizing. I don't know what a general point of view about writing music could be, except that there are certain things I consider very important. One of them is, as I said before, the matter of convincing continuity: one must have that above all other things. Now, how you teach students to accomplish this I really don't know. It's a matter of an almost subconscious . . . taste. Certainly it is not a matter of mechanical application, although sometimes it might seem to be that because in advanced techniques, where so many different musical problems are posed, it's very useful to have a plan or frame by which everything is more or less controlled, so you don't have to start every composing session from zero, faced with the million possibilities now open to us. Only recently I was at a modern music festival with another former student of Nadia Boulanger, and we got to talking about the perplexing problems of writing music nowadays; I said, "Well, you know, you have to start by deciding what the first note is going to be—will it be middle C? . . ." And she said, "Oh, no—it can't be C!" For now you cannot escape the feeling that all the decisions have become so personal that, really, there's very little you can communicate pedagogically except the general sense that whatever music you write, it must have a convincing continuity. But once composers, even reputable ones, start writing pieces with fragments of Mozart and Bach stuck in the middle of them, then what can you say? And if these are part of accepted music, what can you teach? *

* Of course it is true that there are quite a number of examples in which music of a different style is integrated into the flow of music of a quite advanced rhythmic and expressive nature. Bartók's parody (of Shostakovich?) in the Concerto for Orchestra, or his waltz fragment in conventional style inserted just before the end of the Fifth Quartet, or the very

Yet one never hears of music being taught from this point of view of time-continuity, which you feel is so basic.

I remember somewhere Hindemith made a statement that musicians understand everything about music but rhythm. And it's certainly true that the timing of music is somehow a sub-conscious thing, because it's obvious that some good composers have a very different sense of timing than others. For this reason it's probably impossible to teach.

But that this is even important, not to say constitutive, is not even raised as a problem in most cases.

Yes, and this strikes me as funny in the case of the post-Webernians, because it's so obvious that the very thing that makes Webern's pieces interesting on their microscopic level is exactly the same thing that makes longer pieces in more "continuous" style interesting. Thus say, at the climax of the first of the Webern Bagatelles, Op. 9, the contrast of a rapidly rising minor sixth immediately followed by a slower descending minor ninth becomes significant not only because of the way these are related in pitch, surrounded as they are by pizzicati that fill in the characteristic harmony of the movement, but also, more importantly, because of the way they are related "dramatically," by the place they occupy in the time-continuity. The fact that so many "post-Webern" pieces are nothing but mechanical-additive series of these microscopic Webern-like ideas shows that this has never been thought about.

It's obvious, too, that all too often tonal music is analyzed in a time-vacuum, without concern for any but atomistic point-to-point chord relations.

---

subtle introduction by Berg of the Carinthian folk-melody and of Bach's harmonization of *Es ist genug* into the Violin Concerto, are all more or less effective. Ives's quotations of anthems and the like, on the other hand, have their charm, but more often than not they disturb the musical thought of works such as the *Fourth of July* (where an interesting attempt is made to write a sort of mixed-up chorale-prelude on *Columbia, the Gem of the Ocean*) or the "Hawthorne" movement of the *Concord Sonata*. This kind of potpourri treatment (now justified under the name of "collage") communicates little musically—perhaps more programmatically.

This raises the whole question of musical analysis, especially that of contemporary music. It has long seemed to me that the only way to analyze a piece meaningfully is to begin *not* with anything that "exists" on paper, but with the detailed impression that the piece makes on an intelligent listener after many hearings. Any analysis of music has to be the analysis of the means by which a piece makes its expressive point and produces the impression one has of it. Thus any analysis presupposes that the piece to be analyzed is *worth* analyzing, in that it does in fact communicate something esthetically *before* one studies the printed score.

Today it's obvious that there are many "pieces" involving techniques that can be described in a fascinating way, which nonetheless communicate nothing at all. It is unfortunate, therefore, that so much is written about "pieces" whose only interest is the article that gets written about them or the classroom "analysis" that someone does of them, because in this way students often learn a lot of "techniques" that can never be used to communicate anything, simply because they never *were* so used, and were apparently never thought of as means to such an end. This not only confuses talented students but allows a great many untalented ones to think that by manipulating a set of formulas they are composing something, and soon results in the production of many worthless things, which end up usurping a good deal of the limited performance time available to contemporary composers—time which could much better be spent on more thorough preparation of good works.

It often seems that music is taught like bricklaying, and that students are all too rapidly led to putting this and that chord together without having been given any conceptual awareness of the possible relations between kinds of musical event-continuity and kinds of affect—an awareness that would help them keep in mind what they were trying to do as composers with all the different materials now available to them.

Although even bricklaying can have its fascination, as in the difference between the *opus reticulatum* and the *opus quad-*

ratum of Roman architects—which, however, in their day were covered over with marble facings! Too often, what you call musical bricklaying neither has the total effect as design of the Pantheon or Hadrian's Serapeum, nor functions as a support for an interesting surface. Like pedantic archaeologists, it's very easy for music analysts to have that kind of mindless concern for mechanics and formulas in any sort of mass-teaching situation. One thinks of the Bauhaus and its legions of "artisans" turning out "Klees" and "Kandinskys" according to a set of rules formulated by these artists, who taught there. It gets to be like an assembly line.

I must say I was very impressed by this problem when Ravi Shankar, during a speech in the 1930s about how much more interesting Oriental music was than Western music, spoke about the introduction of music schools in India. In the old days a man studied with a guru for ten years or more; but with the coming of music schools and a system of notation, everything had been reduced to rules in a book. And he said, "You know, now music is no longer the same."

This is apt to happen any time art gets reduced to a method for the sake of convenience. That is, every time someone figures out a set of "rules" to explain a musical phenomenon or to try to help other people deal with music in some way, the fact that the rules are, on occasion, somewhat relevant to the subject (often they aren't even that) leads many, teachers and students alike, to consider these "rules" the central thing, the "key" to the thing they're supposed to explain. The "rules" then quickly get mistaken for the thing itself, which soon puts an end to that kind of art.*

* Despite this, of course, there is a very interesting kind of historical development to be considered here: the influence of the codification of artists' practices not merely in reducing the style and practices to routine, but more importantly as furnishing training and often a springboard for the next, perhaps antithetical, style. Four centuries of avoiding parallel fifths in Western music, let alone Fux counterpoint and Rameau harmony (whose relations to actual practice were very indirect), must have left an indelible effect on musicians for the first fifty years of this century, if only to make them very interval-conscious, just as Cherubini's pontifications on counterpoint had their effect on all fugal writing in the nineteenth century, except for the radical few who followed Reicha. Then, too, it is interesting

What is always required is a teacher who can show how particular musical techniques have been used in order to produce certain musical effects and communications, always insisting on this means-ends relationship. This is difficult to accomplish and requires a special kind of gift on the part of the teacher. Nadia Boulanger had this gift, and I will never forget how she illumined the works we studied in this way. Such individuals are rare, however.

Beyond the study of techniques in *good* musical works of the past, whether distant or recent, the matter of learning to compose remains in large part an individual problem. The most a good teacher can really do is try to help the student composer develop a sort of alter ego that listens to his music as if he were someone else, critically, understandingly and not too sympathetically—an alter ego that is not interested in or fooled by effects used in the work or tricks that exist only on paper, but one that listens as the composer himself listens to one of his fellow composers' works: hoping to find something fine, beautiful, imaginative, and gripping in them (but unfortunately not seldom being disappointed).

By way of conclusion, I might say that the very matters of teaching and learning composition begin to appear in an odd light today, in view of the place of serious music in the social developments we have been witnessing since the Second World War in America and elsewhere. These are accompanied by an increasing emphasis on publicity as a means of communication, by a growing tendency for the consumer, engulfed as he is in commercial publicity, to answer back in the same "newsworthy" terms—dress, behavior, mass approbation. One could say that one of the mixed blessings of the music profession is precisely that it is so recalcitrant to the kind of publicity so necessary to the mercantile world and its more vociferous opponents. Besides being hard to exploit commercially under present American copyright laws, serious music lends itself poorly to the "media," since it is visually relatively uninteresting and hard to

---

to notice the migration of the "diabolus" from the augmented fourth (most dissonant and most ambiguous interval during common-practice centuries) to the perfect octave (the blandest and most unambiguous of intervals) during the strict twelve-tone era of the twentieth century.

talk about intelligently and simply. So its production and dissemination defy all the familiar laws of supply and demand. You might almost say that the playing and hearing of it were acts of non-cooperation with our society (even though such acts, by some kind of ritual concept of culture, are still sometimes highly subsidized).

This special situation may mean that the whole profession will die out, or it may mean that it is one of the last refuges of the humanistic spirit. Certainly serious music cannot be explained on pragmatic grounds or on the simple level of entertainment, since in its present state it requires skills, feelings, awarenesses, and intelligences that are increasingly hard to consider worth developing even among a small portion of the population, in spite of the money being lavished upon it.

As has often been said, modern composition often seems to be no longer a public art, since in most places—certainly in America—the public is no longer held together by a consensus about what culture is or what its value can be unless it is "sold" this continually by the mass media, which rarely happens for serious music since it is commercially unprofitable. So the composer is left to his private world more than ever before, to follow whatever seems important to him. His music is highly unlikely to seem very important to many others—perhaps to some colleagues and some of a small public. If he is lucky like Bartók or Ives, he will be recognized by a larger group posthumously, but who can count on the future? But it is just because of these things that the field of composition is so interesting and such an adventure today, since it puts such a special burden on the composer alone. He is freer to write what he likes here at present than he has been in many centuries or even at the present time in Europe, let alone the Soviet Union, and freer than in any Oriental country, where patterns of each traditional music are so constricting and the new is often accepted uncritically as part of the march forward toward "modern civilization." Of course, as I have said several times, the social and economic censorship of serious, new American musical efforts prevents these from ever reaching a large public, unless a newsworthy gimmick is found.

Viewed in another way, music does have one advantage over

almost all other human activities that may be important for the future. It keeps people active, busy, productive, and stimulated imaginatively, without harmful or especially wearing physical effects on them, and it produces no physical residue or pollution. It passes the time, rewarding with a wealth of civilizing (sometimes not so civilizing) experiences, helping us to envision qualities of life and social cooperation that seem to many worth striving for. When machines put us all out of work and we are all on welfare with nothing to do, it may come in handy for those who like to be active.

Bibliography

ARTICLES BY *Elliott Carter*

Numerous reviews in *Modern Music,* issues from Jan.–Feb. 1937 to Winter 1946.
"American Figure with Landscape" (Henry F. Gilbert), in *Modern Music* XX/4 (May–June 1943), 219–25.
"Charles Ives, His Vision and Challenge," in *Modern Music,* XXI/4, (May 1944), 199–202.
"Music as a Liberal Art," in *Modern Music* XXII/1 (Nov. 1944), 12–16.
"Gabriel Fauré," in *Listen,* VI/1 (May 1945), 8–9, 12.
"Walter Piston," in *The Musical Quarterly,* XXXII/3 (July 1946), 354–73.
"An American Destiny" (Charles Ives), in *Listen,* IX/1 (Nov. 1946), 4–7.
"The Rhythmic Basis of American Music," in *The Score,* 12 (June 1955), 27–32.
"Music of the Twentieth Century," in *Encyclopaedia Britannica,* Chicago, 1957, XVI, 16–18.
"Variationer for orkester," in *Nutida Musik,* IV (1960/61).
"Shop Talk by an American Composer," in *The Musical Quarterly,* XLVI/2 (April, 1960), 182–201; reprinted in P. H. Lang, ed., *Problems of Modern Music,* New York, 1962, pp. 51–63.
"The Milieu of the American Composer," in *Perspectives of New Music,* I/1 (Fall 1962), 49.
"Letter from Europe," *idem,* I/2 (Spring 1963), 195.
"Expressionism in American Music," *idem,* IV/1 (Fall–Winter 1965), 1–13; reprinted in Boretz and Cone, ed., *Perspectives on American Composers,* New York, 1971, pp. 217–29.
"The Time Dimension in Music," in *Music Journal,* Nov. 1965.
"A Further Step," in Gilbert Chase, ed., *The American Composer Speaks,* Baton Rouge, 1966, pp. 245–54.
Chapter II, in Robert Stephan Hines, ed., *The Orchestral Composer's Point of View,* Norman, Oklahoma, 1970, pp. 40–61.
"Conversation with Elliott Carter" (with Benjamin Boretz), in *Perspectives of New Music,* VIII/2 (Spring–Summer 1970), 1–22.

WRITINGS ABOUT *Elliott Carter*

Abraham Skulsky, "Elliott Carter," in *American Composers' Alliance Bulletin,* III/2 (Summer 1953), 2–11.
Paul Collaer, *La musique moderne,* Brussels, 1957, pp. 267–68.
Richard Franko Goldman, "The Music of Elliott Carter," in *The Musical Quarterly,* XLIII/2 (April 1957), 151–70.
Richard Franko Goldman, "Current Chronicle: New York," in *The Musical Quarterly,* XLVI/3 (July 1960), 361–64.

Michael Steinberg, "Elliott Carter's 2. Streichquartett," in *Melos*, 1961/2, pp. 35–37.

Joseph Machlis, *Introduction to Contemporary Music*, New York, 1961, pp. 588–96.

Kurt Stone, "Problems and Methods of Notation," in *Perspectives of New Music*, I/2 (Spring 1963), 9–26.

Igor Stravinsky, *Dialogues and a Diary*, New York, 1963, pp. 47–48.

Wilfrid Mellers, *Music in a New Found Land*, New York, 1964, pp. 103–21.

Martin Boykan, "Elliott Carter and the Postwar Composers," in *Perspectives of New Music*, II/2 (Spring–Summer 1964), 125–28; reprinted in Boretz and Cone, eds., *Perspectives on American Composers*, New York, 1971, 213–16.

William Austin, *Music in the 20th Century*, New York, 1966, pp. 442–44.

Eric Salzman, *20th Century Music: An Introduction*, New York, 1967, pp. 172–73.

David Hamilton, "The New Craft of the Contemporary Concerto: Carter and Sessions," in *High Fidelity*, May 1968, pp. 67–68.

Richard Kostelanetz, *Master Minds*, New York, 1969, pp. 200–10.

Stephen Walsh, "Elliott Carter's Piano Concerto," in *The Listener* (London), 31 March 1969, p. 357.

Kurt Stone, "Current Chronicle: New York," in *The Musical Quarterly*, LV/4 (October 1969), 559–72.

Michael Steinberg, "Carter's Concerto Premiered," in *The Boston Globe*, Feb. 15, 1970.

David Hamilton, "Music," in *The Nation*, March 2, 1970, pp. 253–54.

Index